High On The Vine

Featuring Yooper Entrepreneurs,
Tami & Evi Maki
(Cousins, Thrice Removed)

Terri Martin

Modern History Press

Ann Arbor, MI

High on the Vine: Featuring Yooper Entrepreneurs Tami & Evi Maki (Cousins, Thrice Removed)

ISBN 978-1-7352043-2-1 paperback
ISBN 978-1-61599-786-2 hardcover
ISBN 978-1-61599-867-8 eBook

Library of Congress Control Number (LCCN): 2022903539

Published by
Modern History Press   www.ModernHistoryPress.com
5145 Pontiac Trail   info@ModernHistoryPress.com
Ann Arbor, MI 48105

Tollfree 888-761-6268 (USA/CAN)
FAX 734-663-6861

Distributed by Ingram Book Group (USA/CAN/AU/UK)

Best read when enjoying a glass of wine

Also by Terri Martin

Roadkill Justice: Featuring Yooper Woodswoman Nettie Bramble

Moose Willow Mystery: A Yooper Romance

Church Lady Chronicles: Devilish Encounters

For Middle Grade and up readers

The Home Wind: A Novel

Voodoo Shack: A Michigan Mystery

Table Of Contents

How It All Started

Tami and Evi found themselves seeking warmth from the woodstove in Tami's living room, or as Tami called it, the *parlor*. Having not completely adjusted to life in Upper Michigan, Tami still clung to the notion that manners and social graces accounted for something, and to her a parlor is where one received and entertained visitors. Evi was visiting so therefore, the erstwhile living room was a parlor. Furthermore, Tami and Evi Maki, cousins thrice removed, were *at tea* such as one might be invited to if in England. Interestingly, there was no tea present, but rather a fresh box of white wine, which Tami and Evi frequently pressed into service via the handy spigot located front and center. But for purposes of public information (i.e. gossip), the ladies were having tea.

"These little sandwich things are to die for," said Evi as she popped a third one into her mouth. Tami had made some tea sandwiches with miniature squares of cocktail bread, cream cheese, smoked salmon and cucumber slices garnished with a little sprig of dill. These went down well with their emblematic tea.

"Thank you, Evi, I found it in my *Living High on Tea* book, along with my scone recipe."

"I love your scones, too," said Tami as she eyed the plate of crust-less sandwiches, looking for her next victim. "I

1

wonder what the boys are having for their lunch," she said, as she used a freshly-ironed linen napkin to dab a dribble of wine from her chin.

Tami snorted and shook her head in disgust. The ladies' spouses, Toivo and Eino, were likely engaged in their own emblematic tea somewhere in the woods at the Maki hunting camp. Instead of a tidy parlor with doilies on the armchairs, they preferred a sagging couch that likely harbored enough microbes to destroy the world. Napkins would be absent as would any other tools of civility, such as proper silverware and dishes. Toivo and Eino loathed washing dishes and preferred using their hands as eating utensils. They weren't great about washing their hands either, for that matter. Mostly they used their Leatherman tools (unwashed) as eating utensils and wiped them "clean" on their pant legs (also unwashed except when their wives could confiscate them along with their ratty flannel shirts to throw into the laundry).

Tami took a dainty sip of wine, contemplating the bane of her existence: Toivo, and how she had been, if not tricked, at least misled into marrying the clod. Toivo often had similar thoughts about Tami, though he dared not think of her as the pain in the (bleep) she was, since she always seemed to know what he was thinking or doing. Tami always knew what Toivo was up to (rarely work that involved a paycheck) because he was so *predictable*.

"He's got terrible eating habits," said Tami, just as Evi was poised to consume yet another tea sandwich. "Likely he's eating some fat-laden, sodium-rich junk food—something that doesn't require a fork."

Evi held the tea sandwich inside her mouth without chewing for a moment; she felt as if Tami were studying her. Unfortunately, the bread began to dissolve on her tongue, making it difficult to talk. Eventually she managed to get it down by taking a generous slug of wine.

"As much as I complain, I do care about the lout," Tami said. "I don't want him to keel over before his time. He's never been able to get disability, since sloth-itis is not considered a valid medical condition, so we have to wait for regular Social Security. I, of course, have my small pension from the government. I gave up my career at the post office in Blemishville to move up to this place. God's Country, my foot! More like God-forsaken," Tami said.

"I thought you said the post office closed because of budget cuts," Evi said. There were still six tiny sandwiches on the delicate cut-glass plate. Would it be rude to eat them or leave them? Evi was not as cultured as Tami and didn't know the protocol with such things. She knew it was rude to take, say, the last one, but there were several. Her wine was gone too.

Tami sighed. "True, it did close, but because of my stellar work record, I was guaranteed a transfer—maybe someplace warm like Nashville or Atlanta. There were no transfers available up here. Oh, I wonder how my life would have been if not for that double date we had for Slick and Sally's wedding—remember?"

Evi nodded. How could she forget? It was indeed a fateful night. Toivo and Eino were both cousins *and* uncles to one another and related to the groom as cousins several times removed. They had made a special trip down below the bridge to attend their cousin, Slick's wedding and likely to take advantage of the free booze. The bride (and soon-to-be mother), Sally, was a mutual friend of Tami and Evi's from a water aerobics class they all had taken at the fitness center. Sally, matchmaker that she was, fixed Tami and Evi up with Toivo and Eino for purposes of wedding escorts. The boys had cleaned up pretty well and neither Tami nor Evi were getting any younger. Tami, out of vanity, did not wear her glasses, which normally dangled on a decorative chain round her neck, so Toivo's image was somewhat fuzzy and rather hunky. Evi spent too much time at the punch bowl, which was spiked. While doing the funky chicken to a rag-tag band called the Pizzlesticks, Tami and Evi got caught up in the festivities and before they knew it, found themselves somehow enamored with a couple of backwoods reprobates who decided they needed women in their lives to do the cooking and cleaning and whatnot. Before Tami could wipe the fog off her glasses and Evi could sober up, a quick double ceremony took place and Tami and Evi found themselves living in remorse in the back woods of Nowheresville.

"I think the first thing is to cut out meat," said Tami.

"Huh," said Evi, snatched back from her reverie of Slick and Sally's wedding reception. And the party after the reception. The full moon, stars in the sky. The bed of Eino's pickup. Her angry daddy. Mama crying…

"Of course, the boys like to think they are putting meat on the table with all their hunting prowess, but truth be told, Toivo hasn't gotten a deer or even a squirrel for that matter since we've been married," Tami said.

"Well, Eino did get a racoon last spring when it was coming out of hibernation, but it was with his truck not his gun," Evi said. "It was too flattened to salvage any meat but he did use the fur to make a coonskin hat."

"Not much better with fishing either," Tami said. "Though he sure has enough invested in gear. We should have a freezer full of fish."

"Eino got a turtle a while back. It was a snapper. They are good eating, but I refuse to clean something like that. Besides it escaped before Eino could figure out how to dispatch it. Even spit out the hook, neat as can be with the worm still attached. The worm was a little worse for wear."

Tami shuddered a bit. "Yes, meat must go. Also, dairy. The time to eat healthy is when we are still, well, fairly young. We'll be glad we did when we get in our golden years."

Evi looked at the tea sandwich that had somehow made its way between her thumb and forefinger. "Is cream cheese dairy?"

"I'm afraid so," Tami said.

"What about the salmon?" Evi said, rather mournfully. She had developed a real liking to the smoked salmon that Tami procured from the fish market.

"A true vegan does not consume products from or eat anything that walks, crawls, swims, hops or flies," Tami responded.

"Vegan? What's a vegan?" Evi asked. Is that one of those cults?

Tami ignored her. "Nope, no meat, fish, seafood, cheese, milk, ice cream..."

"No ice cream!" shrieked Evi. "I love Mackinac Island Fudge. I must have it..."

"Too much fat in the dairy. And all those chemicals they use to make the animals grow up faster and fatter."

"But fish?" Evi said, still hoping for a smoked salmon exemption.

"Well, do you really want something that swims around in a lake polluted with its own excrement?" Tami responded.

"But *I* swim around in the lake all the time," Evi said. She had never really thought about all the fish poop in there.

"Yes, think about it. I prefer a nice pool where I can see the bottom."

"But there are *chemicals* in the pool!" Evi said, enjoying a small victory for her side.

"True," Tami said. "But no excrement."

"Oh really? What do you think those children do during family swim night?" Evi said ever so smugly.

"That's what the chemicals are for," Tami snapped.

High On The Vine

"Maybe they should raise fish in swimming pools," Evi said.

Tami ignored her. Sometimes Evi came up with the most ridiculous ideas. Still, it did seem that something that was being constantly washed, albeit not always in pristine water, might be better than say a rutabaga. After all, didn't vegetables grow in the dirt? Just exactly what was dirt, anyway? Ground up rock, pollution, contamination, toxins, and of course excrement from all creatures that walked, crawled, flew, or slithered across the earth, doing their business randomly and repeatedly. Why, farmers even *intentionally* put excrement on their crops to supposedly enrich the soil. Ug! Tami shuddered at the thought.

"Perhaps salmon could be an exception," Tami said, as she took a miniscule sip of wine. "Especially if it's smoked. That should certainly purify the meat."

"Oh, absolutely!" Evin said, eagerly nodding her head. There were now three sandwiches left. Okay, two. She had to tip the box to get the wine to flow properly.

"And really, dairy doesn't come from the flesh of the animal. Weren't we all first given dairy from our mother's milk when we were babies?" Tami said. "I would think that having dairy is very natural to us. Even if we add a bit of sugar and some chunks of chocolate."

"Did you know that chocolate is actually a health food?" Evi said. There was one lone sandwich remaining of the plate. The wine box was empty and Evi was feeling a bit woozy.

"Really, how so?" Tami said. She was skeptical that chocolate was "healthy" but felt it important to occasionally let Evi have her say. After all, Tami believed that being a good listener and pretending that the other person had anything of value to offer was simply a social grace that one must exercise from time to time. Even if the other person was, well, *simple,* not to mention beyond tipsy.

"Oh yesh. You shee the chocolate bean..."

"I don't believe chocolate is a bean," Tami said. "It comes in bars. Beans are things you soak overnight to make soup, not fudge."

It seemed that Evi's wine glass was again dry. She was feeling plucky and had read an article in some magazine at the doctor's office about the health benefits of chocolate and she did not believe a doctor's office would sponsor rubbish. She was feeling a bit lightheaded yet emboldened by the wine. "Yesh, eventually it turns into bars, but it sharts out ash a *bean* that growsh on a tree. It has good stuff called flapan-doodles or antiaccidents—or shomethang like that."

"Oh, come now, Evi. Chocolate grows on trees?" Tami snickered. "Is this some wild version of Jack and the Beanstalk?"

"Huh?" Evi said.

"You know," Tami said. "Magic beans?"

"Oh riiiiight! They're mashic. And I want them in my icesh cream. But as fudge, not beans." She giggled. "Beans, beans the musical fruit, the more you eat the more you..."

"Evi!" Tami admonished. "How many glasses of wine have you had? And the sandwiches. I never had even one."

Evi seemed to be snoring. Tami shook her head and sighed. Evi was a dear; she just had a short attention span. Simpleminded, but nonetheless a good friend who simply could not hold her—tea.

Ruminating the Female/Male Conundrum

Tami and Evi sat by a warm fire in Tami's parlor, which by most standards was simply an ordinary living room, but Tami was intent on maintaining a certain standard so therefore it was a parlor. The women were sipping "tea," which came out of a box with a spigot, discussing their husbands, Toivo and Eino. While men discuss their women with a locker room mentality, women become philosophical about their male counterparts, trying to inject sense into them who have none.

The gals' menfolk had gone ice fishing, leaving Tami and Evi in blissful male absence. Glorious hours with no mud tracked in, no toilet seat up, no crumbs scattered on the kitchen counter and no flatulence. Toivo and Eino, who couldn't be bothered to get up by 9:00 a.m. on Sunday morning to attend church, had arisen at 4:00 a.m. to drive out to the bay, trudge across the frozen tundra, cut a hole in the ice and sit in a freezing ice shanty under the pretense of bringing home the bacon a/k/a fish to the family larder. Whether or not the fish were biting was of little concern to the pair, who would remain huddled in their shanty like a couple of dolts, watching their hole skim over, while keeping warm with alcohol.

High On The Vine

Tami topped off the women's wine glasses, added a log to the wood burner, and shared an article that she read in some guy magazine called: *Man Up!* The article discussed the differences between men and women, with women emerging unfavorably as being overly preoccupied with shoes, children, beauty products and miscellaneous details that, in Tami's opinion, is what keeps their households from collapsing into ruin. It was clear that the so-called reporter had overindulged in an adult beverage to have written the defamatory article, which lacked any truth or fact whatsoever and was clearly written by a man who did not see a clear picture at all when discussing the Female/Male Conundrum.

Evi had brought along some lovely scones she had purchased before coming over for her visit with Tami, and the two women nibbled on them while thinking about the actual and verifiable differences between men and women. Oh sure, both sexes have their little quirks. For example, while a woman will excavate deep into the dairy cooler for the freshest milk, a man will grab anything without even checking the expiration date. Unimaginable, but true. It's amazing more people don't die from expired products because of this. A woman will painstakingly price-compare, while a man will simply grab and go, heedless of cost. Though it's true that a woman may have multiple pairs of shoes in her closet—neatly arranged—a man will have a jumble of mud-caked boots moldering out in the garage for everyone to trip over.

Of course, women do obsess a bit over their wardrobes, trying to be attractive and accessorized. Men, on the other hand, NEVER get rid of a single piece of clothing. Ever. There is a reason that the thrift store has an overabundance of women's and children's clothes, and very little men's. The only reason that any male clothing is there at all is because the man who owned it died and his poor wife had to slog through forty- or fifty-years' worth of clothing that is so old it's turning to dust.

Ruminating the Female/Male Conundrum

Along that same line, a woman may have a vast assortment of products, well organized and stored in the bathroom. The man also has his share of things, but they are mostly empty tubes, crusty toothbrushes, combs and brushes that have never been de-haired or de-loused, and of course a lot of facial by-products—whether trimmed or shed—in the bathroom sink. While there is a ridiculous claim in the article that women have 337 items stashed in the bathroom (clearly an exaggeration brought on by intoxication), Tami and Evi point out that the average Yooper male has no less than three boats, a dozen guns, two dozen fishing poles and rods (with extra reels), six tackle boxes containing at least 337 lures, melted/fused rubber worms, five pounds of sinkers, an enormous snarl of tangled fishing line and hooks, and fishing rule books dating back to the Ming Dynasty. This is not to mention duck blinds, tree stands and decoys. And everything has to be "camo" including underwear and sleeping shorts. A woman's meager possessions, none of which were purchased at full price, pale by comparison.

But it isn't the material differences that Tami and Evi contemplate while sipping their wine (Tami has brought out a fresh box). Additionally, being a good hostess, Tami prepared a nice salad for lunch, which featured smoked salmon (store-bought, with an excellent freshness date) and some little orange slices, grape tomatoes and toasted almonds, all resting on a crisp bed of romaine lettuce with a side of a homemade raspberry vinaigrette dressing. Toivo and Eino, to the knowledge of the women, had liverwurst sandwiches, barbeque pork rinds, venison jerky and beer for their ice shanty repast.

Tami hypothesized that the female/male differences reach beyond the obvious physical disparities and transcend beyond the iteration of variation in taste and priorities. No, it is deeper than all these things. The women grew silent for quite some time, listening to the crackle of the wood stove and drinking their wine.

Tami clucked her tongue and shook her head. She thought maybe it was simply a matter of the male Y chromosome, and that men were hard-wired to behave as Neanderthals. Evi nodded. Yes, her Eino did have a protruding forehead and a lot of nasal hair. Tami speculated that those of a spiritual mind and who think that God has a sense of humor, believe that He first created man, found His creation flawed, and sought to salvage the human race through the creation of woman. (Note: the prefix "wo" means "better than" man.) Hence, having confidence in the females (after all He entrusted them to bear young), God left the less-than-perfect male component of the human race around for the females to straighten out.

Tami and Evi sighed in unison. So much work, so little time.

Flush and Flourish

Tami found the position to be rather undignified: down on her elbows and rump in the air, but she was resolved to make things work even if it killed her. She could hear Evi grunting a bit. Evi was a tad overweight. Well, so was Tami, for that matter, but she was used to physical hardships. After all, she was married to Toivo.

"Squeeze! Squeeze! Squeeze!" cried Madam Zanacks.

The idea was to squeeze one's buttocks while thrusting the adjoining leg out, up or sideways. It was all part of Madam Zanacks "flush" operation, which preceded the "flourish" portion of the regime. Flourishing, apparently, involved the purchase of many assorted items sold by Madam Zanacks, which included a colon cleanse, essential oils, herbal teas, age-defying creams, and a CD of monotonous music—such as that being played during the flushing exercise—that would put a cheetah on steroids into a trance.

"Now rest!"

Everyone belly-flopped onto their exercise mats.

"And streeeeetch!

Everyone lay motionless, pretending to stretch. The music was some kind of penny whistle that apparently had only two maybe three notes.

"Next, turn over and reeeeeeeeach."

Everyone turned over on their backs and reached upwards.

High On The Vine

"Everything you ever dreamed of is just beyond your fingertips. Try to grab it!"

It seemed a little counter-productive to be reaching for something unreachable, whether one's dreams or one's toes. Tami glanced over at Evi, who looked like a sleep-walker, lying on her back with her arms outstretched. Or the walking dead. Not to be catty, but Evi apparently forgot to look in the mirror before coming to Madam Zanacks Flush and Flourish class.

Tami was thinking that Madam Zanacks, if not an outright fraud, was certainly mean-spirited and opportunistic. Still, Tami had lost two pounds and could bend over to tie her boots now. She had also been relieved of almost $200, thanks to all the products she was talked into purchasing. It was all the fault of Tami and Evi's husbands, Toivo and Eino. Had it not been for their ridiculous camp, Tami and Evi would never have taken the bait for Madam Zanacks "free" first class, which was the hook that reeled the two women into four weeks of hell on earth.

It all started with Tami and Evi's weekly soiree during which they had pondered the meaning of life and, in this case, discussed with disgust Toivo and Eino's Annual Open Maki Camp Party.

"Well, I just don't understand why Toivo spends all of his time out at that disreputable camp," Tami had said as she adjusted the doily on the arm of her lounge chair. "I mean, why wouldn't he want to be here in our lovely, well-appointed home, which I keep neat as a pin? I am an excellent cook and if it weren't for me, Toivo's clothes would rot off his flesh and he would only bathe in the river once in a blue moon."

Evi nodded in agreement. Her husband, Eino, co-owned the very same camp. It was a family hunting camp, with Toivo and Eino being both uncles and cousins. The camp had endured many generations of neglect, fire, flood, blizzards and wifely scorn. The greatest abuse occurred once a year when a hoard of men crawled from beneath their rocks to whoop it up in a drunken event predictably called the Annual Open Maki Camp Party. The cover charge was—surprise, surprise—alcohol.

Tami said, "There were over two-hundred dollars in empties to return to the IGA after the bash. At ten cents each, that's an excess of two thousand cans and bottles of beer. They filled up all of the crusher machines and the manager asked them to go away and never come back."

"That doesn't even account for Wisconsin no-deposit cans and bottles, or wine and distilled spirit empties," Evi said.

"Well," Tami said, "I am certainly glad that that silly annual open camp thing is over. Now maybe Toivo will go back to work and we can fix the transmission on my car—not to mention the furnace, washing machine, vacuum cleaner and broken exhaust fan in the bathroom. I mean a can of air freshener can only do so much."

Tami and Evi's weekly girl time generally entailed eating pastries that one of the women had provided, drinking wine from a box and philosophizing. Usually they emerged satiated, satisfied and a little sloshed. But this time, discontent hung over them like an icy fog from Superior.

"I may be bored because the winters are so long and now that spring is here, I got nothing interesting going on," Tami said as she nibbled a warm scone, fresh from her oven. "I don't know why I let him talk me into moving from Ohio up here to this God-forsaken, frozen, bug-infested wilderness. Something about living off the land. Hah!"

Evi sighed, "Yes, I had a similar sales pitch. Of course, I'm from Minnesota, which is just as flippin' cold and the mosquitos can carry off a full-grown moose." She took a less-than-dainty bite from her scone. "I love the blueberries that you put in these," she said, smacking her lips. "It seems like all I do lately is eat, eat, eat. I'm beginning to feel like a slug that has devoured one too many azaleas."

"I heard that there's a touchy-feely women's class meeting at the township hall," Tami said. "It's called Flush and Flourish. I think it's probably a fancy way of marketing an exercise class."

"I wonder if it's a blubber-busting thing," Evi said, polishing off her glass of wine. "Or maybe they teach that yoga where you stand on your head and transcend your inner yin or yang or something." She reached over and refilled her glass from the handy little spigot on the wine box.

"I have the ad here somewhere," Tami said as she thumbed through the local newspaper, *The Last Sentry*. "It says here: **'Flush & Flourish!'** For women only! Expel the toxins of mind and body. Come in for a spring tune-up; tone your body and tweak your mind with Madam Zanacks. Cast off the husk of doubt and despair that surrounds you and learn to love yourself and the world around you. Tues/Thurs classes May 1-24, 10-11 a.m. $5 a class or $30 for entire session. First class is free! Township hall. Drop-ins welcome'."

They had dropped in only to discover that Madam Zanack's Flush and Flourish class did not allow dropping out. At least not without risking a spell from The Evil Eye that Madam Zanacks was purported to cast upon those she did not favor, such as quitters. Evi was quick to remind Tami of Flo Fudbuster who got The Evil Eye from her mother-in-law. Shortly after the spell was cast, Flo's cell phone had burst into flames, caught the couch on fire and burned her house down. She barely got herself and her three cats out to safety. Better to stick with it than risk it.

"And now, ladies—breath in—hold it, hold it, hold it..."

Madam Zanack's phone rang—a rather bizarre ring tone that sounded like the theme song from the Addams Family

TV series: ba dadada, click, click, ba dadada... "What! When? Crapola!" she muttered into the phone.

They were all still holding our deep, cleansing breath when Madam Zanacks bolted from the room and out the door. They were still holding it—except one or two who had passed out—when we heard her car start (it lacked a muffler) and roar off. They were still holding it when a couple of cops burst into the room, looking for Madam Zanacks a/k/a Babs Brooks a/k/a Betty Bustier, who was wanted for illegal gambling, money laundering, racketeering, tax evasion and selling cheesy medical contraptions to senior citizens.

Tami and Evi were to later learn that Madam Zanack's Flush and Flourish, while cult-like, had been semi-legit, except that Madam Zanacks had no certification in exercise science nor the dispensing of remedies for healing the body and soul. And while Tami and Evi's purchases of herbs, oils and such were nothing but snake oil, the colon cleanse did wonders for Toivo and Eino, who never knew what hit them next time they went to camp.

Gone Wild

"I could just kill him," muttered Tami to her thrice-removed cousin, Evi.

"Me too," Evi moaned. "It was your husband, Toivo's, idea, and you know that my Eino always does what Toivo does. He'd probably follow him onto thin ice. I think he did follow him onto thin ice once. Remember?"

"Twice," Tami snapped. "The first time they just fell through and Search & Rescue had to be called. The second time they were drifting out to across Keweenaw Bay on an ice floe. If those Native Americans hadn't spotted them and taken a boat out, the two idiots' bodies would have washed up onto shore in Canada and we would *not* be stuck in this igloo or Quinzee or whatever it's called freezing our patooties off. Those two share a brain, and it's the size of a walnut. And just as nutty."

Tami couldn't believe that she was spending the night in what was essentially a hollowed-out pile of snow with a doorway one could barely crawl through and vent hole in the roof that was supposed to keep the occupants from suffocating. The "shelter" managed to trigger every phobia a person could imagine, including taphophobia, which was the fear of being buried alive. There was also the fear of freezing to death, which would make being buried alive a moot point. The Quinzee offered little by way of warmth or protection from whatever was lurking nearby. In spite of the unimaginable discomfort of being ensconced in a pile of snow, there was a strong fear of *leaving* it during the darkness of the night—so the experience was a combo claustrophobia/agoraphobia/taphophobia and whatever phobia described an overwhelming urge to kill one's no-good husband.

"I can't feel my feet anymore," Evi whined. "I think they're frostbitten. Maybe even frozen. I also quit feeling my fingers a long time ago. If they don't freeze solid and break off, I'll strangle Eino."

"Humph," said Tami as she shifted in her sleeping bag. "Strangling's too good for them. They both should endure a slow death, just like we are right now."

"What time is it?" Evi asked. "How long until daylight?"

Tami pushed the button to light the dial on her Lady Timex watch. "It's two in the morning. We have hours until daylight."

The two women fell silent for a moment; lost in an eerie silence. Then a robust howling and yipping broke the stillness.

"Oh my God," shrieked Evi. "Wolves! They're circling us. We're doomed. I hope it's quick."

"First off," said Tami, "we're going to freeze to death before the animals can get us. And second those aren't wolves, they're coyotes. Coyotes won't hurt us," she said with a sigh. "They will, however, feed on our frozen remains."

Tami tried to be patient with Evi, but she could be so hysterical about the least little thing. After all, the bush plane would pick them up in a day or two, along with the half dozen or so other women who for whatever reason were on the Wild Woman Adventure in the middle of the night in the middle of winter in the middle of nowhere.

"Oh. Well, it's a comfort to know that we'll die of exposure rather than be torn apart by wild animals," sniveled Evi.

"Well, I'm sure our adventure guides will make sure neither happens," Tami said, wishing she believed it.

"Adventure guides. Hah!," said Evi. "More like female lumberjacks. And I'm not even sure they *are* female."

"They do seem a bit non-gender specific," said Tami. "But they did whip up a good stew last night. Wish I knew what was in it. I'm thinking about writing a cooking column. Maybe with a survival theme."

The two fell silent again. Tami could feel ice crystals forming in her nostrils. The cold was coming at her from all directions. Neither she nor Evi had packed correctly for the outing, which wasn't their fault. The fault was entirely that of their two *you are so dead when we get home* husbands.

"How long until breakfast?" Evi asked. "Did they say we had to go out on the frozen lake and *catch* our breakfast? What? Is there a Denny's or Golden Corral hidden under the ice?"

Tami ignored her. Evi was really a whiner and was getting on Tami's nerves. Tami saw no point in complaining. Nobody was listening. It was better to occupy one's mind by plotting her husband, Toivo's, death. Actually, murder. His demise would be slow and painful. But these things were delicate and she mustn't get caught. She would not do well in prison. On the other hand, no jury in the world—so long as it had a decent number of females on it—would convict her when they found out what her moronic husband gave her for Christmas. While Tami had specifically requested a weekend at a luxury spa resort—she left the pamphlet right out for Toivo to see—she got instead a weekend in the wilderness.

Tami could kick herself for not asking questions when presented with the certificate, which said she was entitled to participate in an All Inclusive Wild Woman Adventure. She had envisioned a *wild* luxury spa weekend just for the ladies, which would feature bubbling hot tubs, facials, essential oils and massages administered by hotties who smelled like a fresh sea breeze rather than a fish left out in the hot sun. She visualized evenings featuring oiled, bare-chested male dancers wearing little grass loincloths doing the hoochie-coochie, and tuxedoed waiters serving delectable gourmet meals and wine *not* from a box. Evi had similarly been fooled by Eino's identical gift. Of course, their squeals of excitement had quickly turned to cries of remorse when they realized that the poorly maintained single-engine plane they were crammed into was headed for the frozen bush rather than someplace warm, *anyplace* warm.

Naturally, Tami and Evi had packed their rolling suitcases with bathing suits, evening gowns (purchased online with free rush delivery because they were prime members), cruise wear, makeup and other necessities for a weekend of pampering. On a positive note, the female lumberjack adventure guides—or lumber-*janes*—had conveniently brought along essential items such as sleeping bags, boots, padded coats, toques, wool socks and whatnot that they gladly rented or sold (cash only) to anyone who didn't have the proper gear. One of the guides offered to swap a pair of Mukluks for Tami's strappy spike-heeled shoes until the she realized that her beefy feet could never—no matter how hard she tried— be jammed in. Fortunately, both Tami and Evi had brought along ample cash in anticipation of generous tipping for the various bump and grind activities they had envisioned. Now their cash was being extorted by two crusty guides who held life and death in their duffle bags of survival gear.

"I need to use the rest room," Evi whispered.

"Oh, for heaven's sake!" Tami said. "You should have thought of that before you zipped into your mummy bag. And besides, there *are* no restrooms in the wilderness."

Evi was silent for a moment, mulling over her options. "So…?"

"Well, dummy, you just have to go find a tree and make do," Tami said. "Take the flashlight."

"What about bears?" Evi said.

"Hibernating. Obviously smarter than us since we're lying awake freezing to death."

"Wolves?"

"They don't attack people. Or so I've been told," Tami said. "Of course, I have heard stories of them circling hunters who were trapped up in their tree stands for days. The wolves worked in shifts. One fellow purportedly died of starvation waiting for the pack to leave and what was left of him was found dangling from his safety tether. But you know guys and their stories. Probably all a myth."

"What about the Yooper Bigfoot!" Evi said with alarm. I bet those were Bigfoots not coyotes we just heard!"

"Nonsense," Tami said. "As much a myth as Santa Claus."

Evi remembered the day she found out that Santa Claus was a hoax. She had been pretty ticked off that she had been so well behaved for nothing. Turns out that it was her Uncle Lempi dressed up as the jolly old elf. Uncle Lempi always smelled like Old Spice aftershave and bourbon. That's what gave him away. She shifted uncomfortably in her sleeping bag. She still had to go. Bad. Truth be told, she was pretty sure the Yooper Bigfoot did exist—even if the witnesses were not entirely reliable. The harry monster was probably out in the woods, just waiting for someone with a weak bladder to venture out.

"So, will you go with me?" Evi croaked.

"No."

"But we're blood."

"And mine is starting to freeze. I'm staying here until spring."

Evi made a soft whimpering noise.

High On The Vine

"Go to sleep."

"What time is it? I really have to go."

Tami ignored her. Truth be told, she had to go too. Only hers was the more serious kind. She often had gastric distress and had looked online and decided that she had an irrational bowel system brought on by stress. Waiting to die of exposure certainly ratchetted up the stress meter. Plus, the lumber-janes, while they didn't have any wine, did have a flask containing some kind of rotgut that they shared. It burned all the way down and now seemed to be mingling with the what-is-it? stew. Tami could feel her bowels begin to grumble and protest. Fortunately, the guides did provide a roll of what they called APT (all-purpose tissue) to each of their wild women adventurers. This was to be used for everything, including what it was intended for as well as cleaning one's fork and tin cup, which were the only two eating implements provided.

"Okay, we'll both go," Tami said.

"On the count of three," Evi said. "One, two ..."

Before she could finish the three-count, a spine-tingling screech filled the night air and reverberated around the Quinzee's interior.

"Mother of God!" Evi said. "Bigfoot!"

"What on earth?" Tami said.

The yipping and howling started up again then faded away.

"Well, there you see," said Tami. "Nature is taking care of itself. I think the, er, coyotes got something for a late-night snack, so we're perfectly safe to venture out."

Neither of them moved.

"What time is it," Evi asked.

Tami didn't answer, knowing the rest was coming

"I really have to go."

With the added stress of the death cry, Tami was not feeling well at all.

"I suppose we could take a peek and see what's going on out there," Tami said.

"You first," Evi said.

"No, you go ahead and I'll, um, cover you with the flashlight," Tami said. She grabbed the cheap plastic flashlight provided by the lumber-janes and flicked it on. An anemic yellow beam flickered across the snowpack and vanished into the darkness.

Evi had unzipped herself from her sleeping bag and crawled to the door and looked out. Something eerie was undulating in the sky. While Tami tended to be the more religious of the cousins, Evi could only think that she was seeing into heaven. Colors danced and rolled across the sky. It had to be heaven. And if it was, then God was not far away. Of course, Evi always had believed that God was watching, but He couldn't have picked a better time to show up.

"Tami, look!" Evi said, moving away from the door.

"No way. I told you to go first," Tami said.

"Tami! It's God—or at least it's a sign from God."

Tami tentatively looked out the door. The light show had picked up and it indeed was spectacular.

"Those are the Northern Lights you dingbat. You know, the Arora Borealis," Tami said. "Haven't you seen them before?"

"Nuh uh," Evi said.

The two watched the light show, which had begun to fade.

"Well, that was something," Evi said.

The distraction had helped Tami's gut ease a bit. She climbed back into her sleeping bag, which had cooled to a brisk minus ten degrees. Evi also crawled back into her sleeping bag, her teeth chattering rhythmically.

"Tami?"

"*What?*"

"Do y-y-y-you th-th-think (chatter, chatter) th-that wa-was ga-ga-God?

Tami did not answer. How could she plan Toivo's excruciating death with all this God talk?

"Tami?"

"Go. To. Sleep."

"Do you think I'll see God again tomorrow night?"

"Oh absolutely," Tami said.

"Ra—really?"

"Uh huh, because you'll be dead after I strangle you," Tami snarled. "Maybe you'll see God before Satan gets you."

Silence.

"Tami?"

Silence.

"Tami? You awake?"

Tami sighed and lit up her watch. It was now 3:00 a.m. Still hours before daylight.

"Hey. Tami. I really have to go."

Operation: She Shed

"Do you think the curtains are too much?" Evi asked Cuz Tami.

"Absolutely not," said Tami. They bring the whole room together. My, but we've certainly made this ol' cabin a lovely little retreat, haven't we?'

Evi nodded. The two women were sitting around a cozy wood stove, but not in their usual place in Tami's parlor. They had the quintessential box of wine perched within reach along with a nice plate of assorted spritz cookies that Tami had supplied for the outing to what once had been Toivo and Eino's camp. Except it was no longer Toivo and Eino's camp, though the boys were not yet aware of this as they were on a week-long Elk hunting trip in lower Michigan—apparently, the chance of a lifetime, or so they told their wives. The story was that they had won the lottery draw hunting vouchers in a poker game. Whatever.

This allowed ample time for Tami and Evi to implement their rather bold undertaking, which was planned during the wee hours of that frigid morning when they were ensconced within the claustrophobic confines of a snow shelter. In between fighting off frostbite and the abject terror of being ravaged by a slathering pack of rogue coyotes, Tami and Evi utilized the slowly passing time to plot a hideous revenge against their spouses. The boys had pulled a very nasty prank on the women by tricking them into thinking they were going on a luxury resort vacation, when such a notion was pure fantasy. Instead, Tami and Evi, along with tropical resort clothes and sunscreen, were flown into the bush for a winter survivalist weekend where their lives depended on two guides who clearly were the result of some genetic mishap.

Tami and Evi had decided, during their wintry machinations, that the standard forms of retribution that women normally inflicted upon men—such as the silent treatment (as if the boys would notice) or refusing to cook (they would get a sack of burgers) or filing for divorce (meh)—simply would not do. Instead, they came up with a plan so diabolical, so devious, that Satan hisself would have been in awe.

That is how they found themselves at Camp Maki—a destination that they had rarely sought. In fact, prior to recent times, Tami and Evi had only been there once, shortly after they had married the two louts, as a kind of test of the new wives' pioneer spirit. The outing had not gone well and the women had demanded their immediate return to civilization where they felt a need to take long, scalding showers and burn their clothing. Normally, the gals adopted a live and let live attitude toward Camp Maki and, while they were careful not to show any encouragement, were secretly pleased when the boys felt the need to "return to nature." With the two reprobates out from under foot, there was less to clean up and the toilet seat stayed down.

However, proper toilet seat placement notwithstanding, Tami and Evi were always a little miffed that their menfolk preferred each other's company to that of their wives and the squalor of Camp Maki to the comfort and cleanliness of their homes. This helped spawn an epiphany of sorts that would surely land a gut shot to the Maki men.

Operation: She Shed. Mission: to clean, purge, and destroy. While exhausting, Tami and Evi found the undertaking cathartic and rewarding. It had all begun with an initial inspection, then they forged ahead as if in battle, taking no prisoners.

Tami had said: "Once we get the three inches of that disgusting crud off the floor—it's like walking on Crisco—we can get some bright rugs to scatter around. I suggest a lot of pastel to tie in with the other soft goods."

The soft goods that Tami had referred to included the previously mentioned curtains, which sported a soft pastel floral pattern and tiers of fluttery ruffles. These were arranged over the four windows of the cabin, plus the tiny window in the door. Tami and Evi had brought along several buckets of cleaning products and, layer by layer, removed the grime from the windows to better enhance the new curtains and allow actual sunlight to penetrate the cabin. The two women had also pulled the mattresses off the bunk beds, dragged them outside and burned them along with the disreputable sleeping bags that had mysterious lumps that, Evi swore to God, moved. These items were replaced with inflatable vinyl mattresses, which could be easily sanitized. Each mattress was made up with sateen sheets, fluffy blankets, and a comforter with the same busy- bloom pattern as the curtains. The bed ensemble makeover was finished off with matching pillow shams and an assortment of complimenting decorator pillows.

But that was just the beginning.

"Well, the curtains do help," Evi had proclaimed when she had finished shirring the valances. "But that horrible couch and nasty recliner! I mean, what do you think that stain is? Is it what it looks like?"

"I have no idea," Tami said, "but burning would be too good for them."

"And what—they don't even have a table and chairs? Just this old door sitting on some sawhorses and broken lawn chairs. Didn't they have a table and chairs once?"

"I believe so," Tami said. "As I recall, they took it out on the lake when they were ice fishing and it fell through along with the ice shanty and all of their gear."

Evi nodded thoughtfully. "Was that the time that someone driving by saw the two dummies clinging to an ice floe and called Search and Rescue?"

"Yes," said Tami. "Well, at least they got a bath in the process," she said, chuckling. "But anyway, that's what happened to the table and chairs. Too bad we can't send this horrid couch and recliner out on thin ice."

"I think it's against the law—you know, polluting the lake and all," Evi said.

"Well..." Tami said.

Evi knew that tone. It meant that Tami was concocting an idea.

"I have an idea," Tami said, verifying Evi's prediction. "How much ice do you reckon is out there? Enough to hold the truck?"

"I guess," said Evi. "There's a few trucks out there along with ORVs, snowmobiles, and whatnot. I think the ice is like a foot thick."

Tami and Evi had made the trip to Camp Maki in Toivo's rattletrap truck whose massive, nubby tires and souped-up transmission would take it through snow, mud and tag alder like it was cotton candy. Toivo was none the wiser that his wife had his "baby," which he had named Big Buck, out at the camp. He and Eino had felt it a good idea to be scarce for a while and had taken Eino's truck (which was at least three months newer) downstate for their stupid Elk hunt. This "cooling off" period, as Toivo had called it had presented a perfect opportunity for the gals to execute Operation: She Shed.

Toivo's commandeered truck was a combo Chevy/Ford/Dodge, depending on what parts could be found in the local junkyard or otherwise. He had fashioned a boon-docking snorkel, which protruded from the engine compartment, and the front bumper was a large, skinned tree trunk lashed on with rope. The windows were gone and the heater and most other non-essential items didn't work, but there was a dandy winch in the truck bed, which worked like a dream. It was with this device that Tami and Evi had been able to pull the seedy furniture out of the cabin (though the couch was tricky and had to be maneuvered).

"Now what?" Evi had asked her cousin.

"Now we head for the lake," said Tami.

"But..." Evi said, then decided to just let Tami do whatever it was she was planning, which seemed to be to tow the crappy furniture out onto the ice. She hoped that there weren't any Conservation Officers lurking about. Before departing, Tami had instructed Evi to grab a piece of plywood from behind the outhouse along with a nearly dried up can of paint and petrified paintbrush.

Big Buck crept out on the ice while fishermen gawked at the strange sight. The couch slid smoothly along with the recliner, now open, fishtailing along behind. Big Buck's brakes complained noisily as Tami ground to a halt at the ice shanty town. She exited the truck, and unhooked the furniture then propped the plywood next to the couch and hastily painted "FREE" on the board.

By the time the women had retracted the winch, both items had been snatched up and installed into ice shanties.

"People will take anything if it's free," Tami remarked. "How do you think the boys got that crap to begin with?"

With 40 years of grime and crud scraped from every square inch of the cabin and the removal of Toivo and Eino's revolting furniture, the next step had been to deal with decades of accumulated man stuff. This included, but was not limited to, broken fishing and hunting equipment, rusty traps, a smattering of dishes, pots and pans, knives—blades bent or broken—girlie magazines dating back to Marilyn Monroe, crumbling posters, outdated calendars, discarded clothing, empty beer cans, food debris, rodent carcasses, defunct fuel canisters, shredded newspaper replete with animal droppings, and a Tupperware bowl with what had once held some kind of food product, now reduced to a revolting mass of mold and slime. The gas refrigerator contained mostly beer, which was removed by the women along with several bottles of pasty sauce and some kind of dried-up meat. There was no stove (yet), and the grease-laden grill, which apparently had been used indoors as well as out, joined the pile of refuse loaded in the back of Big Buck and destined for the dump.

Upon completion of the purging exercise, Tami and Evi began the restocking and refurnishing of Camp She Shed. They hit the jackpot at a trip to the re-habitat store where a load of decent items had just been dropped off after someone's granny had passed on to her reward. A fussy brocade settee and matching wing chairs, which apparently had only been used on Sunday, were purchased along with a dainty Queen Anne dinette set and matching cabinet. They also bargained for a lovely coffee table, which would be perfect for refreshments. Tami figured she could whip out some doilies for placement on the chairs and tabletops, using the pastel colors that adorned a good deal of the cabin. It was Evi who spotted a serviceable two-burner gas stove, which could be hooked into the gas line for the fridge.

The girls replaced the boy's beverages and mystery foods previously removed from the fridge with several boxes of wine, some flavored carbonated drinks, healthy snacks and pastry sweets that could be kept in the freezer for future consumption. Tami and Evi had visited the local thrift store and obtained decent dishes, pots and pans, and cutlery. Since there was no electricity—yet—there was no point in getting a toaster or blender. Tami did find a stove-top percolator, which she bleached within an inch of its life.

When Tami and Evi had ventured out to inspect the privy, they determined its salvation to be challenging. However, after three coats of Pepto Bismo pink paint (inside and out), a tasteful installation of a dried-flower wreath and other wall hangings, mounting of a mouse-resistant toilet tissue holder, battery-operated air freshener, replacement of the existing toilet seat (a stainless-steel model that Eino got at a prison auction and was as cold as the surface of Pluto) with a nice cushioned model, and lastly a generous application of lime down the hole, the cozy little shack seemed almost appealing.

Tami and Evi had pulled off the She Shed transformation in four days, leaving three days to enjoy the fruits of their labors before the fellas came home. While the men were never prone to violence, they were prone to benders. That's what Tami suspected they would do.

"Do you think the guys will do something to destroy our She Shed?" Evi asked.

"Oh, I doubt it," Tami said. "That would require actual physical exertion, which of course they eschew."

Evi was not sure what eschew meant. Tami was putting on airs again. It sounded like eating something or maybe sneezing, which didn't make sense. She'd be damned, though, to show her ignorance.

"I suspect when Toivo and Eino see the camp makeover, they'll be repulsed by its good taste and cleanliness," Tami said, "so I expect that they'll turn tail and never set foot in the place again."

"What do you think they'll do for a deer camp then?" Evi asked.

"Oh, I'm not sure; they'll figure something out," Tami said.

"I suppose," Evi said.

"One thing I *am* sure of though," Tami said.

High On The Vine

"Hmmm?" Evi said, reaching for her sixth spritz cookie. They went remarkably well with the semi-sweet merlot the ladies had been consuming.

"Those two buttcheeks won't be sending us anyplace cold *ever EVER* again!"

"You got that right, sistah!" Evi shouted, clinking her wine goblet against Tami's.

Getting Down To Business

"This place will never be up to its full potential without electricity and indoor plumbing," Tami said to Evi. The two women were sitting in their She Shed, formerly the hunting camp of their husbands, Toivo and Eino. The girls had taken over the camp and converted it from early crud to feminine delight, thus assuring that their spouses would never set foot in it again. The takeover was an elaborate form of punishment in response to Tami and Evi's nightmare primitive weekend in the frozen tundra, courtesy of the aforementioned Toivo and Eino.

Tami and Evi had been staying in their She Shed for some time, fully entrenched in an experiment to see how their beyond-clueless husbands fared in their absence, with the hope that some form of enlightened appreciation for their invaluable wives would emerge.

Evi nodded as she dipped a piece of bread into Tami's famous spinach dip. She quite agreed that electricity and a flush toilet were really not optional. In spite of hardships, Tami had managed to make the dip, which was delish, and it was served in a bread bowl that you could eat in the process. This made very little cleanup, which was a plus in a place with no running water, unless you counted the leak in the roof.

"I'm quite certain that the lake is polluted and I wouldn't use it for washing, let alone drinking. We need a proper well," Tami said.

Evi nodded again—she found that when Tami was on a roll it was best to just nod. She pulled the little spigot on the box of blush wine that the two gals were sharing and watched the lovely pink elixir fill her oversized wine goblet. Evi was not about to mention that they had all the modern conveniences Tami alluded to back at their primary residences. The ladies' strategy to leave their spouses to their own devices was, if not a total failure, at best slow to gain results. Their husbands seemed content to live in squalor, though they had to be getting tired of canned Hormel chili and skunky beer for every meal. The methane build-up had to be reaching lethal levels by now. And while cleanliness was not a priority for the two crumb butts, at some point, it was bound to become clear to them that the dirty clothes did not magically find their way to the washing machine and that there were only so many clean dishes and utensils in the kitchen.

"I have a plan," Tami said as she submerged a dainty piece of bread into the dip.

Evi perked up. "Move back home and let the boys have their camp back?"

"Heavens no!" Tami said. "We need to raise thirty thousand dollars."

Evi sprayed a mouthful of wine onto the coffee table. "Sorry," she muttered. "But what the heck do we need thirty grand for and how do you propose we get it?"

Tami looked thoughtful. "It's a whole new endeavor. A new livelihood as, shall we say, hostesses for a form of entertainment."

This time wine came out of Evi's nostrils. She choked a bit and dabbed at the two rivulets trickling down her chin. "You mean, like an escort service!"

"What?" Tami said, then snorted. "No, of course not. Perhaps rather than call it entertainment I should say it's a kind of retreat opportunity. We could rent this place out for big bucks, but we need to eventually upgrade a few notches. I did some checking. To bring in electric would cost about ten grand. Then the well drilling would be anywhere from two to five thousand. The septic another bundle. Then we'd need to plumb and wire the place, add a bathroom—maybe with one of those Jacuzzi hot tubs—and fix up a nice sauna so you've got a five-star place to rent out for a vacation getaway. We could add a dock and some paddleboats too."

Evi's mouth hung open. Had her cousin gone crazy?

"I have Gaggled some research. People are getting an average of three to four hundred dollars a night to rent out their vacation homes. *Plus* a cleaning fee, security deposit, booking fee, pet fee, insurance fee, boat rental—you name it. We could be raking in the dough!"

"Four hundred a night!" Evi said.

"Yup, plus all the add-ons." Tami eyed her cousin. "So, how much cash do you have on hand."

Evi had been working for the county road commission for years. She started out answering the phones but kept accidentally hanging up on people or forgetting that she had left them on hold. It was no big deal until the supervisor's wife tried to reach him when she went into labor. Apparently, his cell was turned off. Because of the labor union, instead of firing Evi, they did what governments do: they promoted her. They paid for her to get her CDL and turned her loose with a snowplow.

"Well, I've got my 401k," Evi said. "I think I can get a loan on it. I'm kind of worried about my job though, so I probably shouldn't."

"Oh?" Tami said as she took a delicate sip of wine.

High On The Vine

"Yea, see, they gave me this plow truck last winter that kind of pulled to the right and I didn't know it, but I guess I flattened a few mailboxes. Well, okay, pretty much every box on my route. The county is supposed to replace them, and they are pissed off. So, last summer they made me be a flag person. It's the lowliest job. You bake in the hot sun and turn this sign on a stick from slow to stop, slow to stop, for hours. Drivers flip you off and try to run you over and blame you for everything. And there's no place to pee except behind a tree. I mean, that's okay for guys, but not for me."

"So, you might be looking for a new vocation?" Tami said.

"Well, I was thinking about driving a school bus, but they want professional references and a clean driving record. I might have a couple of points."

"But you can get a loan on your retirement?" Tami said, getting the conversation circled back to raising cash.

"Yea, I think up to ten thousand without penalty. I was looking into it to add a bathroom and laundry upstairs. Back home, that is." She looked around the She Shed and tried to imagine anyone paying more than fifty bucks a night to stay there.

"Well, I have a few thousand," Tami said. "Toivo has always let me handle the bank account. Actually, I insisted. Anyway, I've tucked some away. Also, I found out he sold some old antique car called a Woody for five grand. He lost almost half at the casino before I latched on to what was left and put it in the bank. And I've got my retirement from the post office. I think I can get a loan off it too. Then I guess we get a small business loan for the rest."

All this loan stuff was making Evi nervous. She knew for a fact that you had to pay it back in a timely manner, with interest. Her credit card was testimony to that.

"I figure we could rent this place out most of the year, with winter featuring snowmobiling, ice fishing and such, then of course summer you've got your hiking, swimming, fishing, campfires and all the other warm-weather outdoorsy stuff."

"And bugs and bears," muttered Evi. Tami did not seem to hear her.

Suddenly being a flag person did not seem so bad to Evi. Nor did going back and putting up with Eino. She had to tip the wine box to get the last dregs of grape nectar into her glass. The bread bowl and dip were pretty much decimated.

But there was no stopping Tami once she got an idea. "If you figure we rent this place even half the year, that's 180 days times four-hundred smackaroos—and that's a very conservative estimate. Anyway, we'll be looking at sixty grand a year."

This perked Evi up. Her half would be thirty thousand! She could do well on that. No more working in bad weather with uncouth men on road construction and always getting the crappiest job and defective equipment, just because she was female. And maybe because she was incompetent, but who wasn't?

"I'll get us hooked up with one of those online vacation rental sites," Tami said. "We'll start out by getting electric run into the place and not worry about the plumbing just now. We'll call it a 'rustic getaway.' You know, a get-unplugged-get-connected-with-nature angle."

"For four-hundred a night?" Evi said.

Tami gave her a withering look. "Of course not. I figure maybe around a hundred a night to start. Heck, the state parks charge like fifty bucks just for some tiny little cabin. This is much better."

"If you say so," Evi said, then brightened. "So, when we rent this place, we will need to live at home, right?"

Tami sighed. "Yes, I'm afraid so. We will just have to try make do until we can figure something out. You know, we might even be able to expand the operation into a resort and have an owner's residence right here along with some spiffy little cabins. Maybe an RV campground too. The sky's the limit."

"But for now, we just, er, tough it out with the guys," Evi said, trying very hard to disguise the glee in her voice.

Tami frowned. She hated to capitulate to Toivo, who probably had not yet seen his way to become civilized and may or may not have noticed that she was gone.

"Or," Tami said, "I can live with you, and Eino can live with Toivo. After a while we can switch off houses. Sooner or later the guys will crawl to us on their arthritic knees and beg us to take them back and promise to let us mold them into something useful."

Evi gave it a few seconds of thought. "Great! Let's pack."

Turning On the Gaslight

"So, tell me again what it means to gaslight someone," Evi said. She directed her query to her far-removed cousin, Tami.

"Quite simple, really," Tami said as she rearranged the doily on her chair. "It's a form of psychological manipulation."

"You mean like I tell you there's a spider crawling up your back, and when you freak, I yell PSYCH!"

Tami gave Evi a withering look. Really, she loved her cousin dearly, but she was such a trial sometimes. Evi's grin faded and she reached to refill her wine glass from the box of cabernet that the women were sharing along with some buttery, flaky croissants fresh from Tami's oven.

The meeting the women were having, which Tami called a tea even though there was no tea in sight, was taking place in Tami's parlor. The discussion centered around various setbacks and misunderstandings involving their recently "acquired" property, formerly the deer/beer camp of their husbands, Toivo and Eino. The two gals had converted the disreputable shack that housed generations of debauched and slovenly Maki men into a She Shack. The girls had purloined the erstwhile hunting camp mainly to punish their husbands for any number of transgressions, the most heinous being when the boys sent their wives to a survival winter retreat in the frozen tundra rather than a luxurious tropical paradise resort.

High On The Vine

Though Tami and Evi spent a few days in their She Shack leaving their husbands to fend for themselves in their respective houses, the time quickly came to move back to their comfortable homes with such amenities as running water and satellite TV. Evi was ready to forgive and forget the "surprise" winter survival getaway her husband, Eino, had sent her on. After all, he had likely acted under the influence of his cousin/uncle, Toivo. Tami, known to hold a grudge longer than an ice age, reluctantly agreed to allow Toivo to remain in their home when she returned, so long as he remembered, among other things, to wipe his feet, put down the toilet seat, and refrain from drinking milk directly from the carton. She made him sign an iron-clad agreement. In ink.

The gals also moved on to a new phase in their lives as entrepreneurs and decided—mainly Tami decided—to give up their She Shed and offer it for rent to people looking for that family-friendly special get-away-from-it-all experience. Significant income was a certainty, according to Tami. They named it "Rustic Pleasures" on the website where they posted it along with other ads for fancy vacation rentals. Tami's online information may have been somewhat misleading by omission and rather vague on the definition of "rustic."

"When I said we needed to gaslight our tenants," Tami said, "I didn't mean that we would play childish pranks on them, such as your imaginary spider."

Evi spread some homemade thimbleberry jam on a croissant and nodded as she stuffed it in her mouth. "Mulfff, blaft," she said.

"Honestly, Evi, don't talk with your mouth full."

"Mufft," said Evi, swallowing and washing down the pastry with a slug of wine. "I was trying to ask how it came about."

"Gaslighting?" Tami said.

Turning On the Gaslight

"Uh huh," said Evi, licking a bit of jam off her fingers.

"Well, I think it all came about in some murder mystery filmed in the 30s or 40s. The gaslights kept dimming, and an actress, whose husband was trying to drive her insane by dimming the lights and other deceptive activities, told her she imagined it. Pretty soon, she thought she *was* losing her mind, what with the lights dimming and all and nobody else seeming to notice, but it was all a ploy to cover up a murder."

"Uh, huh," said Evi as she reached for another croissant. "So are we going to do some kind of murder mystery reenactment at the cabin..."

"Rustic Pleasures," corrected Tami.

"Right, whatever. Anyway, we can't do that—gaslighting/light dimming thing— because there is no electricity and only gas on the place goes to the propane stove. There are the oil lamps, but when you dim them, you have to stand right there and turn the little knob, and it wouldn't fool anyone."

Tami sighed dramatically and took a tiny sip of wine. She had a croissant on a dainty China plate sitting in front of her, with one small bite missing. Evi wondered if she was going to finish it anytime soon. Evi was starved all the time because she was on some stupid diet that the doctor gave her. Something about being pre-diabetic. She tried not to think about all the wrong things she had eaten and drank that day. Truth be told, she couldn't think of one right thing.

"Anyway," Tami said, "as soon as we get the money, we'll put in electricity. It's going to be a tad more than I thought."

"Yea, like ten grand to run it from the highway up Billy Goat Road where the cabin, er Rustic Pleasures, is. But maybe we could charge extra for the murder."

"We are not having a murder mystery enactment at Rustic Pleasures," Tami said, "though it's not a bad idea to think about down the road."

High On The Vine

Evi grinned. It wasn't often that she came up with an idea.

"All we are doing," Tami said, "is convincing our tenants that certain experiences in the wilderness could be construed as fun, rather than a hardship."

"You mean, like having a snake in your bed or mice in the kitchen and a bear in the outhouse?" Evi said.

"Well, yes, and that doing without modern conveniences builds character, pulls a family together—gets them unplugged and in touch with each other and nature."

"Too bad the first ones came during black fly season," Evi said. "Even though we reduced the price way down to $99 a night, they started right off complaining."

Tami looked thoughtful as she took a second tiny bite from her croissant. Evi watched her cousin absently chew the morsel. Was she even enjoying it? It seemed a waste to eat something if you didn't even notice it was in your mouth.

"Yes," Tami said, "I'm afraid city folks think the word 'rustic' means only 200 channels on the television and no Jacuzzi in the bathroom. If only it had a bathroom instead of just the outhouse."

"And a bright pink one at that!" Evi said. "But our website specifically says: 'path bath' and hand pump."

"Indeed it does," agreed Tami. "When we checked the folks in, the woman seemed, well less than pleased. Apparently, she thought path bath was some kind of spa treatment and her husband thought the hand pump would be in the exercise room. I tried to point out that we didn't charge any extra if they wanted to split their own firewood, which is excellent exercise. The kids were having a meltdown because there was no WiFi or satellite TV. I told them about the games and puzzles that we bought from Goodwill and put up in the Fun Cupboard and they looked at me like I had lobsters coming out of my ears."

Turning On the Gaslight

"I remember," Evi said. "I tried to point out the view of the lake, but the rain and freezing fog kind of spoiled it. The missus was having a hissy fit because her husband uses one of those breathing machines, but it needs to be plugged in."

"I mean, really," Tami said shaking her head morosely, "do we have to spell it out for them? A whole chunk of the website telling them no electricity, no indoor plumbing, no television, no WiFi, and to bring your own sheets, towels, soap, potable water, toilet paper and bug dope? Did they not notice the lovely authentic native stone fire ring we made out there on the beach? It took you, what, an hour to gather all those rocks. And the sign pointing to the hiking trail, well game trail. The swamp can be such fun if you don't mind getting your feet a little wet. Also, there are two perfectly good kayaks that are easy peasy to paddle, though I admit I forgot to purchase the paddles. I mean, shouldn't they come with them? Plus, we have marshmallow sticks in the Fun Cupboard, along with flippers—well flipper—, a snorkel, mask, floating air mattress..."

"Oh, I forgot to mention," Evi said, "I think mice made a nest in the air mattress. It no longer holds air since a large portion has been chewed away. I think the critters used the 1000-piece puzzle for nesting material. I didn't have time to really clean it up and the woman screamed when I was showing her the, er, fun stuff."

Tami slapped her forehead. They would have to spring for a fumigator, not to mention waiving the cleaning fee that was to have been imposed on the guests.

"We need a new marketing strategy," Tami said. "That's where the gaslighting comes in. We need to psychologically convince people that they are having the time of their life, even though they are sucked dry by mosquitos and terrorized by a rogue bear who has learned how to work the combination lock on the front door."

High On The Vine

Evi was feeling a little tipsy and she giggled causing a small trickle of wine to exit her nostrils. "Riiigt," she said. "Convince people that ish fun to suffer."

"That's it!" Tami shrieked. "It's not fun 'til you suffer! Spend a weekend, a week or a month in Rustic—wait not pleasure. Hmmm."

"Hell!" Evi bleated.

"Perhaps too strong," Tami said.

"Hades?"

Tami shook her head.

"Maybe we should abandon the place and let it go wild," Evi said, feeling her eyes droop.

"That's it!" Tami shrieked. "WILD ABANDON."

"Huh! What?" a startled Evi said. It was a good thing her glass was empty, or she would have spilled perfectly good wine.

"Come and live in WILD ABANDON!" Tami reiterated. "Now that, dear cuz, is how gaslighting is done. A clever play on words to entice potential guests and coxswain them away from a few minor inconveniences. I'm glad I thought of it. I'll start redoing the web site."

"Wait a minute," Evi said. "I think I was the one..."

"It doesn't matter," Tami said. "The important thing is that we're a team."

Evi was used to her cousin hogging all the glory. Evi had just figured out what gaslighting meant and now Tami used some vulgar sounding word combining a man part and a pig. Undeniably, Evi was feeling surly because she was starving and maybe had had a tad too much wine. When Tami stood up to start clearing away the "tea" dishes, Evi noticed an enormous spider crawling up her cousin's back. It was black and hairy and making steady progress toward Tami's hair, which she kept in a complicated chignon. Of course, she could yell SPIDER! But then her cousin would think she was just gaslighting.

The Wholey Hideaway

"So, how much did we clear?" Evi asked her cuz, Tami. The two women were having their weekly BEEP (Business Enhancement Entrepreneurial Plan) meeting in Tami's parlor. Their BEEP meetings were similar to their "teas," which involved no tea but rather a chilled box of wine and some sort of delectable treat, which was Evi's favorite part of the meetings/teas. This week's item was buttery thumbprint cookies with homemade thimbleberry jam in the middle.

The business question directed to Tami related to the bottom line regarding the ladies' daring venture of becoming vacation rental hostesses. While Tami had contributed the "brains" to the enterprise, Evi had chipped in a large portion of her retirement fund. Their husbands, Toivo and Eino, had contributed their hunting camp in a hostile takeover by their wives, who originally converted it into their She Shed. Then, seeking an entrepreneurial opportunity, the ladies transformed their She Shed into a vacation rental and first dubbed it Rustic Pleasures and later renamed it Wild Abandon, which was supposed to conjure up an image of living large in the wilderness without benefit of electricity or running water, satellite TV or WiFi.

Tami & Evi learned that the phrase "wild abandon" meant different things to different people, which is why they unknowingly rented to a group of aging nudists who soon discovered that a mosquito- infested woods was not a good place for a clothing-free weekend getaway. Their demand for a refund was met with Tami pointing out that mosquitos were part of nature, and that they, Tami and Evi, were not responsible for acts of nature and that the renters should "put something on—at least some bug spray." Perhaps, however, it would have been better if the group *had* gotten their refund and left. Once a breeze came up and the biting insects were kept at bay, a regrettable bit of timing caused a scandalous incident.

While it was not posted that nudity was forbidden on the beach, that should have been obvious since the Budworm United Methodist (BUM) Church Camp for Wayward Youth was located across the lake. As the nude volleyball game was fully underway, many of the Wayward Youth, who had been provided binoculars, ambled down to the beach for a boring waterfowl-watching activity. While several of the children observed a family of geese bobbing in the water, their binoculars strayed to the vacation rental shoreline where the lively game of nude beach volleyball was taking place—a bouncy sport indeed. The nudists maintained that nudity was how God delivered us into the world and that it was "healthy" for the camp kids to get a gander through the powerful lenses of their binoculars at the assortment of gender parts. The camp director disagreed wholeheartedly. Again, Tami and Evi declared themselves harmless of any liability.

Nudity and traumatized kids notwithstanding, the long-term plan was to turn hefty profits with Wild Abandon, which would then offset the estimated 30K price tag to add such amenities and electricity, running water, satellite TV and WiFi. Once this was accomplished, the rent could rise dramatically along with the social and financial status of the clientele.

Tami cleverly sidestepped Evi's question about the net profits of Wild Abandon by offering another thumbprint cookie. "After all," Tami had lectured, "no reasonable person expects a new business to turn a profit the first year."

"But you said..." Evi began.

"Perhaps I was overly optimistic," Tami sighed. "Isn't that the story of my life? Great expectations followed by bitter disappointment." Tami was, of course, referring to her marriage to Toivo Maki. She had met him at a family wedding reception and had been too vain to wear her glasses, and her blurred vision combined with too much punch led to an egregious misjudgment of character and appearance in her choice of a husband.

"We do need to screen our applicants more carefully," Tami allowed. "Also, I have taken the liberty of changing the name of the rental."

"Again?" Evi said as she held her wine goblet under the little spigot and pulled the lever. An amber stream of peach merlot trickled into her glass.

"Yes, I've already made the change," Tami said. She was holding one of her thumbprint cookies minus the one bite she had taken. Evi had consumed three. She was trying not to reach for a fourth in that her doctor had warned her about her pre-diabetes condition at her last visit. Since the thought of shooting up insulin made her break out in a cold sweat, she declined the temptation of another cookie, even though one had an extraordinary amount of sweet/tangy jam oozing from its thumbprint.

Tami said: "I think we should try to appeal to a more, well, respectable clientele, so I took the liberty of going on the website and changing the name of the rental from Wild Abandon to Wholey Hideaway."

"Holy what?" Evi said.

"It eliminates any ideas of random nudeness and wicked

ways, don't you think?" Tami said. "It's all in the perception. It has a *whole*someness without being overly zealous."

"Holey, as in full of holes?" Evi said. This was not far from accurate as the roof was known to leak, but Evi did not see it as a good selling point.

"No, dummy, as in *holy*, like the Bible, but with a W and an E, so it's a play on words. Get it?"

"Not really," Evi said. She was feeling a little left behind in the whole naming process.

"Like, you know, it's a *complete* hideaway—whole, yet it has a double meaning bordering on religious—holy," Tami said as a *bing* emanated from her pocket. She pulled out the "business" smart phone that she had recently purchased with proceeds from the nudist weekend group.

"Monks!" Tami yelped, startling her cousin and causing her to dribble wine down her leather vest.

"I've got an inquiry," Tami said, squinting at her smart phone. "The Benevolent Brotherhood of Sylvan Monks is interested in having a retreat in a place that has no technological distractions or modern conveniences. They are willing to pay handsomely."

For the first time since the formation of their business partnership, the two women smiled at each other.

"What's a Sylvan Monk?" Evi said, reaching for the cookie with the extra jam in the middle. After all, a small celebration was in order.

Tami began tapping the smart phone to look up the definition. "Well, *silva* means of the forest and according to Wick-a-pee-de-ah, a monk is a Christian man who has withdrawn from the world for religious reasons, and is a member of an order of cenobites, living according to a particular rule and under vows of poverty, chastity and obedience."

"Hmmm," Evi said, chewing thoughtfully. "Obedience to who?"

"To *whom,*" Tami corrected. "I suppose God," she said, taking a miniscule bite from her cookie.

Tami frowned at the phone. "Well, I never..."

"Never what?" Evi said.

"They won't do business with women. It's against their doctrine."

"Well, then no deal?" Evi said, washing the final bite of cookie down with a swig of wine.

"Now wait. Let me think," Tami said, drumming her fingers on the doily-covered tea table that held a genuine reproduction of a Tiffany lamp.

"Perhaps we'll have to clean up our husbands and use them as go-betweens," Tami said.

"Clean up, how?"

"Well, we'll head to Wal-Mart and get them each a non-flannel shirt and some khaki pants. I know after Toivo has a couple of beers, he'll let me trim up his hair."

"Yea, Eino too."

"But we need them to be well-versed in Bible stuff, you know to spout off a couple of scriptures so that these Woodland Monks will hand over their tithes and offerings," Tami said, smirking at her wittiness.

"Yea, sure," Evi said. "Like the fellas would do that for just a couple of beers. Probably not even for my chicken-fried whitefish nuggets."

The two women sat for a moment and contemplated their options. Too much buttering up of their menfolk would be regarded with great suspicion. While sometimes Toivo and Eino seemed a few rutabagas short of a pasty, if they put their heads together, a low-wattage lightbulb might come on and there was the possibility that they'd be on to their wives' scheming.

"We'll have to cut them in," Tami said.

"You mean, like *share!*" Evi said.

High On The Vine

"I'm afraid so," Tami said. "Make them (gag) temporary business partners and give an offer they can't refuse."

"Cash?"

"Right," Tami said. "We'll help them get in touch with their, um, spiritual side then conduct their business with the Forest Monks and insist on the cash up front, which we'll quickly snap up for 'safekeeping.' Then we'll turn around and pay off our hubbies with a modest cut and send them off to the casino or wherever they want to blow it."

"I hate to share, but I suppose it could be worse," Evi said. She wasn't sure what could be worse, but there was always something worse until you reached The Worst-Ever.

Tami began tapping into the smart phone. "I'm telling the monks it's a deal. They offered *TWO THOUSAND DOLLARS* for the week. So much for the vow of poverty. I guess they make money somehow. I heard some of them make jams and jellies to sell to the tourists. It seems the evil ways of the world, such as capitalism and technology, have crept into their lives and the head monk wants to disconnect them for a while. Anyway, they intend to meditate, pray and fast. *And* remain mute and totally cut off from civilization. Hmmmm."

"I've heard that sound before," Evi said. "What are you up to."

"Well, maybe we could convince the boys to join this order of Benevolent Brothers of the Swamp, or whatever they call themselves. You know, trick them. We could offer Toivo and Eino a hundred bucks each as the aforementioned cut if they join the monks—but we won't mention that they're monks. We might stretch the truth a bit and tell them it's a beer tasting/poker convention or something. By the time they figure out that there's no beer or gambling and beat it out of there, me and you could split with the eighteen hundred and have us a nice vacation. You know, to make up for that horrible experience from last winter. You remember, when Toivo and Eino shipped us off to the frozen tundra rather than to a tropical paradise?

"How could I forget?" Evi said, dabbing at the wine stains on her vest. "I still have nightmares about being eaten by wolves."

"Personally, I've always wanted to go to Vegas," Tami said.

"Yea, me too," Evi said, brightening. "Sin City! Woo hoo. They have cheap flights out of Gwinn, I hear."

Tami tapped her phone a few more times. "If we book now with *La Femme* Travel, we can get a package deal for five hundred each called "Women's Wicked Weekend," including the flight, three nights in The Dusty Dollar Hotel along with $100 in casino chips, complimentary breakfast, and LIVE MALE ENTERTAINMENT. After the thousand for our package deals, we still have us $800 left over. I love the slots. Gimme your charge card."

"Why my card?" Evi whined.

"Maxed mine out buying those damn kayaks with no paddles that nobody uses. I'll pay you back my share as soon as we get the rental money. Plus, I'll let you have the window seat on the plane *and* my complimentary beverage. It says the hotel has a pool and spa and some kind of thing where they cover you with hot rocks. A real luxury place, just like we planned way back last winter."

"When do we leave?" Evi chirped as she dug her charge card out of her wallet. (Purses were not her style.)

Tami entered the charge card info into the phone. The two women waited for the transaction to process.

"Wonder if I should get a swimsuit," Evi muttered to herself. "I imagine they don't allow skinny dipping in pools like me and Eino do at the river."

"Success!" shrieked Tami. "We are booked on the red eye a few hours after the Monks arrive. Perfect. Let's go down to

High On The Vine

Heinki's Bar, round up the boys and give 'em some of that ol' time religion."

Evi nodded absently, wondering if she could pull off a skimpy swimsuit. She heard there was lots of shopping besides Wal Mart in Las Vegas. She didn't want one of those boring black swimsuits with the skirt and ruffles designed to hide fat. She was a full-figured woman and proud of it. She reached for the last cookie. Maybe should could find something in leatherette.

Pecking Order

"This time they've really done it," Tami said to her distant yet nearby cousin, Evi, who was pulling the spigot on the wine box that the two ladies were sharing at their weekly soiree or BEEP meeting. The flavor of the week was a chardonnay. Tami wasn't sure if the wine or the bakery offering from Tami was her favorite part of the women's "teatime," which was taking place in Tami's parlor. It was actually just a living room replete with tatting and other fussy adornment and there was no tea in sight or even in the tea cannister in the kitchen for that matter, but for the U.P aristocracy, it was teatime in the parlor.

Evi was still enjoying the afterglow of the cousins' trip to Vegas, where they enjoyed a few days of gambling, overeating, gambling, overdrinking, debauchery, gambling, pampering, and gambling.

Tami, on the other hand had quickly moved from conciliation to condemnation toward the gals' spouses. "Chickens," she snarled. "Those two dirty birds won a bunch of chickens and now expect US to take care of them."

The dirty birds in question were the aforementioned spouses, Toivo and Eino, who had spent a good deal of their lives on earth accomplishing little and committing transgressions too numerous to reconcile even if they lived to be a hundred, which was unlikely.

55

High On The Vine

Evi was licking the homemade icing off her fingers after polishing off a sizeable piece of cinnamon swirl coffee cake. "Mupfff," she responded.

"Honestly," Tami continued in her rant, "we leave them to their own devices for one little weekend while we go to Las Vegas for a little R&R, and they do this. First it was that horrid trip to the frozen wilderness run by that creepy woman lumberjack, or jane—whatever ... that they sent us on last winter, promising it was a luxury spa vacation!"

"And instead of a relaxing massage, we were nearly ravaged by a pack of wolves!" chimed in Evi.

"Why can't they just win cash like normal people when they gamble?"

"Like us!" Evi said, taking a sip of wine. "Like that church lady, um..."

"Bea Righteous," Tami said.

"Yea, we did good at Blackjack and she did at the slots AND we all shared. I'm trying to figure out what to do with my cut."

"Hmmm," Tami said.

"Probably pay off my charge card," Evi said. "Maybe buy me some new clothes. Got my eye on a sweet little leather outfit from "Chaps, Chains and Beyond,""

"But no!" Tami said, ignoring her cousin's questionable taste in clothes. "They win a chicken ranch with 300 squawking, pooping birds and the ranch doesn't even include the ranch at all, but just the chickens, some feed and chicken equipment. Not even the coop."

"Yea," Evi said, and we gotta get them in three days or else they start charging rent. If we leave it up to Toivo and Eino, we'll end up paying rent until the, er, cows come home."

"Hmm, Tami said, "chickens lay eggs."

Evi nodded as she always did when Tami stated the obvious. Even she knew that GIRL chickens laid eggs. Boy chickens crowed, which was annoying and useless unless you were a farmer who needed to get up, well, with the chickens.

"Farm fresh eggs can sell for up to three bucks a dozen," Tami continued to muse.

"Uh huh," Evi said, eyeing the middle piece of the coffee cake. That was the premo piece—the center. It had the most icing.

Tami frowned and took a miniscule nibble from her piece of coffee cake, which she washed down with a delicate sip of wine. "There are logistical issues."

Evi wasn't sure what logistical meant. She heard UPS ads talking about logistics, so she expected that maybe it was something to do with package delivery. What that had to do with chickens, she had no idea.

"The main problem is how to transport the fowl to their new quarters, wherever that may be," Tami said.

It *was* about package delivery! She was right. Evi didn't think that UPS would deal with the chickens, though, maybe the feeder and waterer and nest boxes and stuff, but the chickens she didn't think so.

"We can use Big Buck!" Tami said.

Big Buck was Toivo's pride and joy POS truck, which sported a tree-trunk front bumper, snorkel for "swamping," a mishmash of tires and enough rust to rival Detroit.

"But we can't bring chickens *here*," Evi said, looking around Tami's immaculate parlor. Her focus moved to her empty wine glass, which she placed under the spigot and pulled the lever. When nothing came out, she tipped the box and was able to squeeze out enough to fill her glass one last time. She looked at her watch. Teatime had gone on for two hours and she was feeling a bit tipsy and just a little queasy. She figured it was hunger, as it was almost time for lunch, which she dreaded. She was on a pre-diabetes diet, which basically consisted of starvation. She had no idea what half the fruits and vegetables even were on the list that the doctor's office had provided. For example, kale. It looked like something for rabbits or horses, and it was tough and chewy like gnawing on grass. And kiwi, which was supposedly a fruit, looked like a hairy golf ball. She'd be damned if she'd eat that. Spinach was slimy and made her gag and broccoli made her pass gas. A burger and fries never gave her a moment's grief and she figured it was because her body preferred that to rabbit food.

"There is the shack behind the vacation rental," Tami said, getting Evi's mind back to the "logistical" problem of housing 300 chickens.

"We could convert it to a coop. Maybe we could have the vacation renters of Wholey Hideaway take care of the chickens as a kind of get-back-to-basics experience."

Wholey Hideaway was the name of the vacation rental property cabin that Tami and Evi possessed. It had previously been a squalid hunting camp of the Maki husbands but was seized by their wives and converted into a semi-habitable abode. An earlier moniker "Wild Abandon," had caused some issues when a nudist group wildly abandoned their clothing while renting the cabin and were spotted by children in a youth camp across the lake. The let-it-all-hang-out group was engaged in a bouncy game of nude volleyball on the beach during a time when the kids had been provided binoculars for waterfowl watching. Ugly lawsuit threats eventually diminished and so did subsequent bookings at the rustic rental, which they renamed Wholey Hideaway in an attempt to restore respectability. In spite of setbacks, Tami and Evi still clung to the idea that their vacation rental was a veritable pot-o-gold that would be their ticket out of middle-lower class life.

"We could change the name..." Tami began.

"Again?" Evi said. "The varnish isn't even dry on the sign from last time."

"Yes, we need to make it more countryfied," Tami said. "Kind of a pioneer experience, roughing it in the wild, tending the flock of chickens, maybe learning to can tomatoes and such."

The thought of tomatoes kicked up Evi's reflux and she suppressed a belch. She was getting as bad as Eino, though at least she suppressed her gas issues in a civilized manner rather than flaunting them.

"I know somebody who will fix up the shed and make it into a coop for a couple of cases of beer," Tami said.

"Cousin Heinkki?" Evi asked.

"Yes. I'll give him a call and maybe even throw some cash at him too for a hurry-up job," Tami said.

The women contemplated this next entrepreneurial adventure.

Evi frowned. "You don't think our hubbies will want a cut of the action, do you?"

"Sure, we'll give them a cut, so long as they clean out the coop and get the eggs to market."

Both women burst out laughing at the very thought of their husbands doing actual work beyond tinkering with a beer keg tap or duct taping the hinge on the mailbox.

At first the plan went smoothly enough. Getting the shed at Wholey Hideaway converted into a coop took their cousin Heinkki one and a half cases of beer. He put up shelving for the nesting boxes, cut a door and installed a nice ramp for the chickens to come and go on. They had a feeding area inside the door and outside in the chicken yard as well, with room for several feeders and waterers in each area. Additionally, it seemed wise to create a fenced-in area using over ten rolls of chicken wire and other material for two gates, or the chickens would likely become a snack for the many predators lurking around the cabin. While the feeding equipment was part of the deal, the fencing cut into the ladies' Vegas windfall.

High On The Vine

Finally, just before the deadline, 300 angry birds were loaded into crates and piled next to Big Buck. It took several trips to move the chicken paraphernalia along with the crates of chickens that squawked loudly to express their negative opinion of the ordeal. At last Tami and Evi loaded the final crate of chickens into the bed of the truck. The farmer who lost the chickens to Toivo and Eino in a poker game had a smile on his face when he tied the tottering stack of crates onto the truck with baling twine. His wife stood on the porch glaring at Tami and Evi, as if they were the ones who corrupted her man and made him lose the chicken ranch.

"Well, this is it, er Mr., um," Tami stammered.

"Just call me Earl," he said with a grin.

"So, if we have any questions..."

"You can Gaggle it," said Earl, his grin turning a bit sinister. "I'm shed of this once and fer all. Nice little tax write-off. You gals got you some fine laying hens. Ya also got some that don't lay no more. Them's the ones you cook up fer Sunday dinner. There be a couple of roosters in there too. I calls 'em Beaky and Cheeky, but they don't come when ya call 'less you got some scratch. They's more interested when the ladies are strutting around, if you get my drift," he said winking dramatically. "'Course you don't want no fertilized eggs goin' to market. And it's not the right time to be raising chicks. I recommend you have the roosters for dinner as well. They's nothin' but window dressing. I kept them 'cuz my daughters raised 'em up from chicks and we was sentimental. The girls went off and got married, but we still couldn't bring ourselves to eat 'em. Sides, we got us a freezer fulla meat of all kinds with pig hocks coming out of our ears."

Tami and Evi stood dumbfounded trying to take in all the info Earl was passing along. *Eat* them! How did that work? The women were used to getting their fryers from the grocery store thoroughly dead, plucked and cut up into nice-sized pieces neatly ensconced in plastic wrap, freshness date clearly visible.

"Come git yer supper, Earl, afore I slop it to the hogs," bellowed the farmer's wife from the porch. "I ain't callin' but once," she emphasized this with a slamming door when she went back into the house.

"Gotta go. Supper's waiting. We's having pork hocks, turnips and stewed maters. My favorite!"

Farmer Earl waved merrily as Tami drove the rattletrap truck off the farmstead for the last time.

The two women were silent for a mile or two. If there had been a rearview mirror, they would have seen the trail of chicken feathers fluttering in their wake. But being that both mirrors had fallen off the truck eons ago, they were spared witnessing the wind-whipped plucking taking place.

"Gaggle chicken care on your phone," Tami instructed Evi.

Evi tapped her phone for a few minutes. "There's a lot of information here. We can watch a video or I can read off some of the pointers."

"Well, I can't watch the video while I'm driving. We'll have to do it when we get to Wholey Hideaway," Tami said. "Hey, we still haven't renamed the place. We should get on that right-away so I can change the website and get this chicken business underway."

"Nothing's coming to me," Evi said as she stared at the screen of her phone. "They talk a lot about chicken poop in this chicken care link. Apparently, chickens poop in their water, food, on their eggs and occasionally on each other. We're supposed to clean it all on a *daily* basis to keep our birds healthy and happy."

"How about "Chicken Cabin," Tami said, ignoring the mounting bad news about the feeding and care of chickens.

"Or Fowl in the Forest? That's kind of clever, don't you think?"

"Also, you need to clean out the nesting boxes because there will be poop in them along with slimy broken eggs with—" Evi squinted at the screen—"what looks like feathers stuck to them."

"Or how about "Birds of a Feather?" Tami said, feeling a bit unsettled as she rounded the corner onto Goat Path Road where Wholey Hideaway or whatever the new name would be was located."

"And apparently you don't need roosters," Evi continued her tutoring. "They are more trouble than worth and can injure the hens when aggressive."

"Pecking Order!" Tami blurted.

"Yes, it also talks about pecking order," Evi said, "and you need to cull the birds that bully the others."

"No, dummy," Tami said. "As a name for the rental. Pecking Order. Clever, huh?"

Evi shrugged. "I guess. Doesn't make it sound like much fun, you ask me."

Tami nodded. "You're right. We need just the right name to reel in the guests."

Beyond exhaustion, the gals stared ahead, their minds not coming up with any catchy new name for the rental.

Plain and Simple and Eventually Rich (maybe)

"So, what's the name of the family that's renting the chicken ranch?" Evi asked her cuz, Tami, as they nibbled on deviled eggs. Well, Tami nibbled and Evi popped the whole thing into her mouth at once. Actually, several times. There were a lot of eggs in both Tami and Evi's fridge these days, being that their n'er do well husbands, Toivo and Eivo, won a truck load of chickens in a poker game. The Maki women, under a deadline to remove the chickens from the original owner's premises or pay "board," had transferred the fowl to temporary, now permanent, quarters at the erstwhile Maki hunting camp, cum vacation rental, and now makeshift chicken ranch. Neither of them had any experience with chickens, other than those that were defeathered and ensconced in plastic wrap for display in the meat section of the IGA, where all products that previously roamed the earth were guaranteed to be GMO free, drug free, free range, cage free, free of everything, except free to leave.

While Evi was on her second goblet of festive cranberry wine, Tami took her first sip, and seemed to contemplate its worthiness, even though wine snobbery was generally not appropriate when the product came from a spigot attached to a cardboard box. Nonetheless, Tami expected things to always be of the highest standards for the Maki BEEP (Business Enhancement Entrepreneurial Plan) meetings.

"Yoder," Tami answered. The new chicken ranch tenants are the Yoders."

"They're oddish, right?" Evi asked, as she popped a third deviled egg into her mouth. She enjoyed Tami's bakery items much more, but deviled eggs did go well with cranberry wine. Besides, her doctor had warned her against too many sweets as she teetered on the edge of diabetes. Eggs were protein, which was good.

"Not oddish, Amish," Tami corrected. "Honestly, you dingbat, you will get us in trouble if you insist on using marginalizing names. Try to be more politically correct and maybe you should go easy on the wine."

"Sorry, but you have to admit that they are—odd," Evi said.

"Well, odd or not, they are the perfect tenants for the chicken ranch," Tami said. "We are truly blessed that they came our way. I think that asking Bea Righteous to pray for us was smart and it worked! I'm sure that old biddy has a direct line with The Man Upstairs."

"Who?" Evi said as she trickled some more cranberry wine into her goblet while giving her cousin a defiant glare.

"Oh, for heavens' sake, Evi, The Man Upstairs is a euphemism for God."

"A what?" Evi said, reaching for one of the three remaining deviled eggs.

Tami sighed in exasperation. "Anyway, finding a tenant who eschews electricity and running water is truly a miracle!"

"They chew electricity?" Evi said. "How much wine have you had?"

"Eschew, you ninny. It means... oh, never mind. Anyway, their religion mandates they lead a simple and plain life and shun the outside world."

Plain and Simple and Eventually Rich (maybe)

Evi knew the meaning of shun all too well. She had personally experienced it many times. A prime example was during the blizzard of '18, while working for the Stump County Road Commission, she inadvertently obliterated every mailbox on her snowplow route. Was it her fault that the plow truck pulled to the right? That had earned her a shunning and demotion to summer "flag person," where she baked in the hot sun for eight to ten hours a day in various God-forsaken construction zones while turning a sign endlessly back and forth from slow to stop. For her efforts she received the finger, vile language, and garbage thrown at her by frustrated motorists. The upside, however, was that Evi had injured her wrist turning the sign back and forth a million times and now she enjoyed a nice disability check every month. At least for a while.

"So, anyway," Tami continued as she took a tiny bite of her deviled egg, "they are happy to live in the cabin, albeit rent-free, as caretakers."

Evi paused mid guzzle and choked a little, causing some cranberry wine to dribble out the corners of her mouth. The vision reminded Tami of Dracula after a blood-sucking episode. "Rent free!" sputtered Evi. "I thought we were charging $400 a week plus cleaning fee."

"That was before we obtained all those damn chickens," Tami said.

"Still... free?"

"Yes. All eight of them..."

"Eight! There's only four bunks and..."

"Yes, there is the husband and his wife and their six children, ages zero to seven. Also, I think another may be on the way."

"All in that tiny cabin?" Tami said, eyeing the empty deviled egg plate. She wondered if there would be something else to eat, as it was nearly lunch time.

"Well, Mr. Yoder is putting up an addition of two bedrooms. And he's fixed up the loft for the boys. Also, they're building a better outbuilding for the chickens and their three horses, four pigs, and the milk cow..."

"Holy Moley!" Evi said. "That's a lot of livestock. I still don't see how we..."

"Let me finish," Tami said. "Anyway, the Amish help one another. I was not aware but there is quite a community of them around here, and they are going to all do some kind of a barn raising—or at least a shack raising. Yoder is paying for the materials and I'm giving him a five-year lease, for a dollar and other good and valuable consideration."

"What is this 'other good and valuable consideration?'" Evi said, sure that the world could hear her stomach growl.

"See, that's where we get rich—or at least reasonably well kept," Tami said.

"I'm listening," Evi said, liking the get rich part of the conversation.

"Well, the Yoders are going to run the poultry business. They do all the work, buy all the feed and whatnot, and split the profits with us."

"Split, how?"

"Why, fifty-fifty. Mr. Yoder is a very crafty businessman. People like to think that the Amish are not interested in making money, but they do quite well, I am told."

"So, how much?" Evi said.

"Well, it's hard to say at first, because while we don't have to bother with the feed and maintenance and all, those are business deductions that take place before the profits are calculated and divvied up. But I figure we should make at least a thousand bucks a month. More or less. That's figuring one egg per hen per day, plus, er, meat sales for those who don't keep up with the quota and of course the roosters who do nothing much but crow."

Plain and Simple and Eventually Rich (maybe)

In spite of the rather depressing fate for a certain sector of the chicken population, Evi was keen on hearing more about the profit margin. "Each?" she asked. "A thousand each?" Evi was due to have her wrist examined in two months to see if she could return to work with the Road Commission and she had a sinking feeling she would be released to return to work, which she dreaded more than a tooth extraction.

"More or less," Tami said rather evasively. "But wait, there's more!"

"More to eat? You don't by any chance have any croissants lying around, do you?" Evi said hopefully.

"Well, in a way, more to eat. No, Toivo ate all the croissants, with sardines on them of all things. Anyway, it seems that Mrs. Yoder is quite a cook. Most of the Amish women do know how to lay out a spread, but Mrs. Yoder— Hannah is her first name—is beyond even the Amish standards of haute cuisine. Of course, pride is not allowed, so she is very modest. Nonetheless, she has agreed to collaborate with us in creating a cookbook."

"Cookbook?" Evi said, curling up her lip. "There's a million cookbooks out there. Everyone goes online now and Gaggles recipes."

"We'd go hard copy and e-book. That's why Hannah needs us. She's not allowed to deal with computers. I've already thought of a name for it: A Thousand Plain and Simple Ways to Make Chickens Cheap."

"A thousand recipes!" Evi said.

"Well, maybe it should be like a hundred ways. Anyhow, the Amish are sometimes referred to as 'the plain people' who espouse a simple life. So, the title captures that. And, again, we'd split the profits fifty/fifty. I figure twenty bucks a book—cheaper online since we don't have the printing costs—and we could easily clear another thousand a month."

High On The Vine

"Each?" Evi said. She was feeling a bit tipsy. Probably from starvation. The fact that the cranberry wine box sat dead empty had nothing to do with it.

"Well, sure, each. Eventually. More or less," Tami said.

"Good," slurred Evi. " 'cause I chew going back to that job of turning the road sign back and forth."

"Well, you can just tell them where to put that road sign!" Tami said cheerfully. "We're going to be rich, plain and simple."

The Chicken &
the Egg Enigma

It wasn't Tami's "parlor" that Evi was sitting in having "tea" and it wasn't wine from a box that she was drinking. Indeed, the beverage that she had been offered was, ironically, actual tea. And she didn't care for it particularly, but politely sipped it. Evi noticed that Tami, who was sitting across from her at the enormous table built to accommodate the large Amish family, was drinking her tea like it was an everyday thing. In fact, Tami had extended her pinky finger in a delicate fashion as if this were high society, when, in fact, the accommodations were anything but posh and actually downright primitive. Nonetheless, Tami was always one to put on airs.

Evi, on the other hand, considered herself "authentic." Even the vest and pants she wore were genuine simulated leatherette. Tami had scowled at her when they had left their homes to visit the chicken ranch. Apparently, Evi's attire did not pass muster with Tami who was wearing a rather dowdy dress. Evi figured that Tami's drab choice of attire had something to do with their business meeting with an Amish woman, Hannah Yoder, the co-author of the soon-to-make-us-all-rich cookbook *Chicken or the Egg? Recipes, Amish style*. It was a working title that Tami had concocted.

High On The Vine

"Well, this is quite lovely," Tami said as she took a tiny sip of tea and nibbled on a sugar cookie. In spite of her doctor's warnings about her blood glucose, Evi had succumbed to several of the sugar cookies, which were the best cookies she had ever tasted, including the secret family recipe for butter cookies passed down by Evi's Finnish ancestors.

Tami and Evi had gladly vacated their homes to get away from their spouses, Toivo and Eino, because the boys were, once again, launching some ridiculous plan for something neither of their wives cared to know about, likely involving hunting, fishing or gambling. They did know for certain that their husbands weren't pursuing anything that might produce a paycheck.

Hannah Yoder was standing at the propane stove in the cabin of the chicken ranch, cooking a large batch of chicken garlic stew. The cabin itself had been the Maki family hunting camp, until a hostile takeover by Tami & Evi who had converted it first into a girls' getaway, then a vacation rental, and now to house a large Amish family that was tending the flock of chickens that Toivo and Eino had won in a poker game and, ultimately, left for their wives to deal with. In that the former hunting camp lacked amenities, such as electricity and running water, and that the Amish lived a plain life, the match was made in heaven, or thereabouts. Tami and Evi both had to admit that the Yoders had done a lot with the place, adding two bedrooms and fixing up the loft into sleeping quarters for the Yoder boys. They had also torn down the old shed and built a new barn to house the chickens, some cows, pigs and several horses.

The smell of the chicken-garlic stew hung heavy in the overheated kitchen, making Evi a little nauseated. A young boy and girl, who seemed to match in age and may have been twins, eased their way into the kitchen. The boy, wearing a white shirt, suspenders and dark pants eyed the sugar cookie plate. The girl was wearing a printed dress, apron and little white cap like her mother. She gazed at Evi and reached out to touch the shiny leatherette pants. Hannah Yoder snapped something in German and the girl snatched her hand away. More German jibber jabber, and the two children left.

"You must excuse them," Hannah said, "they don't see many English."

"Well, we Maki women are mainly Finnish, with maybe a little Norwegian mixed in," Evi said.

"You goose," Tami said to Evi. "They call all outsiders English."

"Uh, why? Evi said.

"Taste!" Hannah said, holding a large spoon of the stew in front of Tami, who took a tentative sip and smacked her lips. "Why, Hannah, it's delish."

Evi was thinking that the abundant smell of garlic wafting around the kitchen would certainly keep vampires at bay, not to mention anyone else within a 20-foot radius.

"Now don't tell my Rebekka—that's the saucy child who felt your leg—that her pet chicken, Clucky, is in the pot. That one, always making pets of the livestock. She pouted for a week when we butchered her little piggy, Butterball."

"You ate the girl's pet pig?" Evi blurted out.

"Oh no," Hannah said, as she stirred her bubbling stew. We traded the meat for some parts to fix the manure spreader."

Tami gave Evi a reproachful look. Evi didn't care. As a girl she had had a pet goldfish named Mr. Finn and knew how attached one could get to pets. Besides, meat came in plastic wrap in the case at the grocery store. The whole ordeal was making her a bit queasy, just like hunting time at the Maki homestead. That and the fact that there was such a thing as too much garlic.

"So, I write the makings of my stew down on paper and you put in our book?" Hannah said, handing Tami a crumpled piece of lined paper. "So sorry about the gravy stains," she added.

Tami squinted at the scribbled sheet of paper. "Is this in your German? I'm having a little trouble, er, what is a boy of least?"

Hannah chuckled and took the paper back, looking at it for a moment. "Oh, I'm so sorry. Bad handwriting. It's a bay of leaf," she said handing it back to Tami.

"Ah, bay leaf, I see," said Tami, handing the sheet to Evi who was trying to snatch it from her. So far there had not been one penny forthcoming from the chicken ranch venture, and the cookbook scheme was beginning to look a bit shaky. Printing costs alone were astronomical and doing a cookbook online was not as simple as one might think.

"Do we really need to describe how to kill and pluck a chicken?" Evi said. She wondered if "boy of least" was in the tea as well as the stew. She was actually feeling a little giddy *and* urpy.

"Oh yes, that way the meat is very fresh!" Hannah said.

"Well, perhaps when we do this online," Tami said, "we could have a link to the process of converting a, um, live chicken into a stewed chicken."

"Link?" Hannah said.

"We'll show you later," Tami said. "Just keep up with the recipes."

Evi was looking at the other ingredients. No surprise that it contained six cloves of garlic. She wondered how many people still kept lard in the pantry or fresh-shelled peas or home-canned succotash, whatever that was.

There was a loud thumping as the household patriarch stomped into the kitchen. The odor of manure comingled unpleasantly with the garlic chicken aroma.

The Chicken & the Egg Enigma

"This is my husband, Thomas," Hannah said. "Thomas, meet Mrs. Tami and Mrs. Evi Maki. They will be helping with the recipes."

Thomas was the grown-up version of his son, wearing a white shirt, suspenders, dark pants and he clutched a tattered hat and well-worn barn coat in his grimy hands. Mr. Yoder had a beard but no moustache, which looked odd, as if he couldn't decide about facial hair. Thomas, apparently a man of few words, nodded and grunted, hung his coat and hat on a peg by the door and moved to the sink to wash up. A kitchen hand pump had been installed to make water fetching a breeze. A mob of children swarmed in from all angles, with two of the older girls supporting toddlers on their hips. The entire brood came to a screeching halt when they saw the Maki women.

"Children, these ladies are Mrs. Maki—both of them are Mrs. Makis. They will be our guests for lunch."

There was a crash from the sink. Thomas Yoder jerked around and looked sternly at his wife. Tami was pleased to see that Hannah held her ground. Evi was really beginning to feel lousy. She was sure it was the tea and the garlic, manure and swarm of rug rats milling around her.

"Oh, well," Tami said. "We wouldn't dream of intruding, we'll just..."

"Of course they will leave, these English," said the doubting Thomas.

The children all piped up their objection begging that the Maki women be allowed to stay. One boy clung to Evi's leatherette leg, running his hand up and down it's smooth surface.

Sharp words in German snapped all of the children to attention who began taking seats at the enormous family table. An older boy brought a couple of extra chairs from somewhere. Thomas was still trying to assert his authority by standing rigidly by the sink. Hannah gave him a shove toward his seat at the head of the table. "*Dat,* you want to show the children it is good to love and respect all, not just our kind," she hissed. "It is God's will." He appeared to slump a little and slid into his chair, bowing his head. Everyone bowed their head.

"We will honor our guests," Hannah said, "who will give us a prayer of thanks to God."

"Er, really I, couldn't," stammered Tami. "Evi?"

"Yea, sure. Um, hey there God, thank you so much for this bountiful, er, family and food. Please make our book successful. In Jesus' name we pray, eh? Amen."

Everyone chorused *amen.* Thomas glared disapprovingly at Evi while Hannah dished up the chicken garlic concoction and a well-orchestrating counter-clockwise passing of the repast took place, which in addition to the heaping bowls of stew, included plates of bread, butter, jam, a pitcher of iced tea for the adults and milk for the children. There was no chatter during the meal, just the clinking of spoons and subtle slurping noises. Since it was Saturday and there was no school for the kids, Evi wondered what they did all day.

"Well, Hannah, this is just delicious food." Tami said. An awkward silence followed with Thomas Yoder casting a stern look at Tami while the children all giggled. Thomas turned to Tami. "We thank God for the food and are not prideful nor do we welcome compliments."

Well, if he doesn't just suck all the air out of the room, thought Evi.

"Now Thomas," Hannah said, "we must know what is good and what is not in order to sell a recipe book. Do not be rude to our guests."

Thomas, clearly enraged at being chastised by his wife turned a bit red, rose from the table with his chair scraping loudly and stalked to the peg where his coat hung. "Boys, it's time for chores."

The boys all grabbed slices of bread and what was left of the sugar cookies and hurried after their father.

"Well!" Tami said. "I never!"

"Never what?" said a girl looking to be of the tween years. In spite wearing no makeup and plain clothing, she was clearly going to be a beauty.

"Quiet, Ruth, don't hound our guests," Hannah said.

"Oh, not at all," Tami said. "It's an expression, is all—Ruth. I was just a little shocked that your father stormed out like that."

Hannah and some of the girls had begun to clear the table and wash the dishes with water heated on the stove. Hannah said: "Thomas feels, well, less a man that I make money selling the eggs along with some bakery items to the English tourists and local stores and now perhaps do a cookbook with Englishers. Selling to tourists—to outsiders—is nothing new to us, but Thomas is always afraid it will get carried too far."

"Speaking of eggs," Evi said. "How is that going? How's the ol' bottom line looking?"

"Bottom line of what?" said Ruth the tween.

"She has so many questions," Hannah said. "Speaking of eggs, it is time for the daily collecting."

Tami and Evi looked at each other and rose from the table.

"Perhaps we could witness this collection process, so we can understand more about, er, expenditures," Tami said. "You know, the cost of things before the *profit,* which we are splitting 50/50. Just wondering about our part of the split."

"Oh, yes, it is time to discuss business." Hannah said. Girls, you go start getting the eggs collected. The Mrs. Makis and I have some grown-up talking to do."

Once the kitchen was empty of youth, Hannah went to the door, locked it and pulled down the shade.

"I could not do this with anyone around, because of blabbing little mouths. And Thomas—well, he works hard but has no head at all for business. I pretend that I know nothing, but of course that is not true. And it is a tradition that the wife gets to keep the egg money for discretionary spending. And there is a lot of egg money."

"Oh, really?" Tami said.

"Tell us more," Evi added.

Hannah went over to a hutch that contained the family's nicer things. Some China, a pair of candlestick holders, an oil lamp, some figurines. She pulled open a drawer and lifted out several tablecloths. Next, she slid back a panel in the bottom of the drawer.

"Nobody knows about this secret compartment except the Miller women. That was my maiden name, Miller. We have always had our little secrets from the men. My grandmother hid poetry and fine literature books from her husband, as he didn't think women should read anything but the Bible. My mother hid two decks of cards that the ladies used to play pinochle when they were supposed to be quilting. She kept a little cash there, too—just in case. They think they run the show, men, but—anyway. It's all here, after buying the feed and other things. It will be good to get rid of some of this."

With that Hannah pulled out armloads of cash all neatly bundled. Tami and Evi's mouths gaped at the sight of the stash as it tumbled onto the table.

"So, now, we split it up 50/50. Let me get you a bag to carry out your part. Also, I'll send you the leftover chicken garlic stew for your men—it will make them, er, manly— along with some fresh eggs that the girls are gathering," she said. "I also have written down three more recipes of chicken dishes and an egg breakfast bake," she said, shoving more crumpled paper at them.

"Now I hope you do your part and get this cookbook going. I am saving up a college fund. I do not care what

Thomas says. My oldest, Abraham, he is finishing high school. Most Amish children only go through the 8th grade. But my Abraham is going to graduate this year and then go to the veterinary school at Michigan State University to be an animal doctor," she said as she counted out the money. "He has the way with the critters and we have so few veterinarians for large animals anymore. Thomas is afraid he will go to college and never come back. I know my Abraham. He will come back because, of course, he has agreed to be baptized when he is eighteen. Mostly, though, he has a girl who is very special who will wait for him," she said, handing a bulging canvas bag over to Tami. "Count if you wish, but I think it is equal. I will take my share to the bank and put in the college account next time I go to town."

"I—I don't know what to say," Tami said.

That's a first, Evi thought as the chicken stew and mysterious tea roiled about in her stomach. If each bundle was, say, $50 to $500—well it made Evi's head spin. Then she smiled. No more standing out in the broiling sun at road construction turning the blasted "slow/stop" sign! She had been assigned that duty after hitting a few crummy mailboxes when driving a POS snowplow during the winter of '18. She snorted when she thought about her farewell to the fellas at the road commission. She hadn't forgotten how they had put a coiled rubber snake in the women's toilet for her to find. No, she sure hadn't. And the dead spider in her lunchbox, and the deer antlers in her locker and the bags of shredded paper in her car. Lots and lots of bags. She was still finding little pieces of paper in every nook and cranny of her vehicle and pieces still flew out of the vents when she turned on the heat. Perhaps, as a farewell gesture she could do something interesting with the road sign...

Famished

The Maki cousins were engaging in their weekly fireside chat in Tami's parlor when Tami, who was without question the Alpha female, turned to Evi and said: "Evi, I need some advice." Not Evi's opinion, mind, but advice.

This called for a quiet mini celebration on Evi's part. She slipped her wine goblet under the spigot of the wine box that sat perched on the doily-shrouded coffee table. The grape flavor of the week was a merlot. Evi approved and found the sweet, fruity taste much to her liking although, admittedly, she pretty much could drink anything. Truth be told, she did not have the discriminating taste of her thrice-removed cousin, Tami, but she did have a preference for sweet versus dry wine. Of course, wine snobs always went for dry, like somehow drinking something that made your face pucker defined good taste. Hah! These were the people who pretended to like kale and broiled fish. Speaking of food, Evi was pleased to see that Tami had made a loaf of bread that utilized several eggs along with a batch of tartlets filled with prune and almond paste and topped with an egg wash.

Eggs were in abundance in the Maki households due to the conversion of their husbands' erstwhile hunting camp into the now chicken ranch being managed by the Amish Yoder family out on Goat Path Road, and stocked with fowl won by their numbskull hubbies in a poker game. The Yoders were comfortable with the lack of amenities at the chicken ranch and effected multiple improvements, while turning the chicken and egg business into a booming enterprise from which the spoils were shared between Hannah Yoder and Tami and Evi. While Tami opted to do some home improvements, Evi spent part of her windfall paying off her credit card bill and then put merchandise back on her credit card with purchases from her favorite fashion outlet: Chains, Chaps and Beyond.

Now fortified with a bit of the grape, Evi anxiously awaited learning what advice Tami was seeking. Perhaps she wanted to change her hair color or paint the parlor (living room to anyone else) or decide what to do with her lout of a husband, Toivo, who was at that very moment off with Evi's lout of a husband, Eino, supposedly looking for seasonal work. Tami and Evi were not fooled. Toivo and Eino were likely at the local tavern drinking beer and talking about any number of things, none of which included work. In any event, they were out of their wives' hair, which was satisfactory at the moment.

"I am thinking about becoming a newspaper columnist," Tami said.

Well, you could have knocked Evi over with a chicken feather. Never in her wildest imagination had Tami thought Evi would want to write for a newspaper, or that a newspaper would want her to write for them for that matter. Before she could utter a response, Tami continued.

"It would be a weekly recipe column," Tami said. "I mean, we have all of these chicken and egg recipes in our cookbook. Why not expand our readership?" Tami and Evi had entered into an ancillary chicken/egg venture with their Amish partner, Hannah, and published a hard-copy and online version of a cookbook entitled: "Chicken or the Egg? Recipes: Amish Style."

"I am sure," Tami continued, "that you have noticed that *The Last Sentry* lacks anything about recipes or anything else that might interest women for that matter."

Evi nodded. It was true. The local newspaper featured dull write ups about board meetings, syndicated political columns, sports, and disturbing full-color photos of dead creatures that previously roamed the earth or swam to waters of Upper Michigan. There was nothing for women except an occasional ad for a church bazaar where Tami sold a lot of doilies that she tatted throughout the year.

"So, what do you think?" Tami asked.

Evi knew that Tami wasn't really asking for advice and contemplated playing devil's advocate. After all, what was the point? The chicken and egg cookbook was selling like, well hotcakes. She had to admit that the tartlets that Tami had prepared for their fireside chat were delish. One would not think that prune/almond paste would be so pleasing. She loved the way it oozed around on her tongue up to the roof of her mouth.

Tami was looking expectantly at her parlor mate who had just crammed a tartlet into her mouth in order to give herself time to think. Evi pretended to look thoughtful then swallowed the tartlet. She refilled her glass, pleased to note that the box was still alive and well. Evi always got bold after her third glass of wine.

"Does *The Last Sentry* know that you plan to write this cooking column?" Evi asked. "And, I mean, what's in for us? Newspapers don't pay beans."

"It's all about the exposure," Tami said. "And I do know the editor, of course, Tom Spin, who is a fourth cousin on Toivo's side."

High On The Vine

Evi nodded and took a thoughtful sip—actually gulp—of wine. She was dismayed to note that her goblet was empty. Tom Spin had once done an article on Evi entitled: *One Woman in a Man's World*. He had picked Evi because she originally drove a snowplow for the county—until the unfortunate incident during the Winter of Twenty-Eighteen when her POS plow took out a few, actually, about four-dozen mailboxes. Thereafter she was demoted to flag person during construction season, a vocation that she was hoping to soon ditch if the egg business continued to flourish.

"I also know Tom's wife, Helvi, who is in my tatting circle. I'm sure she'd put in a good word for me. I have been giving her farm-fresh eggs at a deep discount."

Everyone in the Village of Budworm knew how henpecked Tom Spin was by his wife so it was a safe bet that Tami's idea would come to fruition.

Evi nodded and refilled her glass. She noticed that Tami had barely taken a sip or two from hers. While there was egg bread left, the prune tartlets were gone. Evi wondered about the impact of all those prunes as she felt a rumble deep within her gut. "What will you call your, er, column?"

"I've been thinking about that," Tami said, "but am a little stumped. I mean, we could stick with the chicken and egg thing, but it won't always be recipes for chicken and eggs.'

"How about 'Whatchagot Cookin' Good Lookin'?" Evi said with a slight slur. She was pretty sure that she had too much prune paste and would need to visit the room down the hall.

"Hmmm," Tami responded. "I was thinking of something a little more, ah, dignified, like 'Northwoods Recipes' or 'Country Cooking.'"

Evi yawned. *Boring* she thought to herself. "Whatever. Will Hannah Yoder be part of this."

Tami took a sip of wine and looked thoughtful. "Oh, I don't know. Her husband is such a control freak. And of course Hannah has been great, but we have a lot more Finns than Amish around here, so we need to be mindful."

Evi thought about Finnish food, such as the gelatinous lutefisk and disturbing squeaky cheese family recipes that she endured as a child. She hadn't minded the Nisu bread that was made palatable only because of a generous slathering of icing.

"I suppose it could be a combination of the two," Evi said.

Tami furrowed her brow a moment, then brightened. "Of course! We can mix the artery-clogging Amish cooking with the bland of the Finns to come up with a whole new genre of food!"

"Famish," Evi said, slurring noticeably.

"How can you be famished?" Tami responded. "You ate a dozen of my tartlets and a half loaf of bread. Not to mention several glasses of wine."

Evi tipped the wine box and squeezed the final dredges into her glass. She was having trouble focusing on Tami. "Noo, shilly, th' name fer th' newshpaper thingy. FAMISH. Shee you..."

"Oh! I see," said Tami. "You combined Finnish and Amish and came up with Famish. I must admit that is clever Evi."

"Shank yoush," Evi said, feeling her eyes droop.

"Famish Cooking!" I'm calling up Helvi. I'll take her some eggs and some tatting patterns and ask her to talk to Tom. Evi?"

"Huh?" Evi said, looking through slit eyes at her cousin.

"Did you hear what I said?" Tami asked.

"Shuur," Evi said.

"So now we need to think of our first recipe," Tami said. "Just to get things started until people start sending recipes in."

"Uh hun," Evi said. "Habout butter cookish. My gran made good uns. Gramps loved 'em 'til he died."

"Well, perhaps," said Tami. "It would be nice to have a kind of combo of both the Amish and Finnish."

"Shikken fried panna caa coo!" exclaimed Evi.

"I beg your pardon?" Tami said.

"Ya know, that Finnish pancake thing, only fried. The Amish fry everything—even vegetables."

"You mean Pannukkau?"

"Yesh!"

"Fried?"

"Yesh!"

"Sounds dreadful. Keep thinking."

Evi realized that even though she was blotto from too much wine and sugar, she was really the creative one of the two cousins. If there had been any wine left, she would have toasted to herself. "Finn alm mash flim flan famine," she burbled.

"That's it!" shouted Tami, momentarily startling Evi out of her stupor.

"Whash it?"

"Famine stew!"

"Wha?"

"It's perfect!"

"It ish?"

"Yes. It can be frugal yet tasty and nutritious!" Tami said. "Probably chicken parts, rutabaga, carrots, tomatoes, hot sauce, garlic, onion, chili powder..."

Suddenly Evi didn't feel so hot. She struggling to her feet. "Now, ish yule 'scuse me, I gotta visit...

Tami watched her cousin stumble off to the powder room and clucked her tongue. She took a thoughtful sip of wine then stood and headed to the kitchen to make up a batch of Famine Stew for Toivo who would likely arrive home in a totally inebriated state. Tami mentally continuing her list of ingredients and while rat poison came to mind, she only considered it briefly.

High On The Vine

"So, they just left?" Evi said. "I mean, no reason given—the Yoders just packed and left!"

Evi had posed this question to Tami, during their weekly BEEP meeting in Tami's living room cum parlor.

"Oh, Hannah said some lame thing like they were moving to Southern Michigan—Sturgis, I believe—to run a cheese business that they apparently recently inherited. Well, actually, not really recently as I guess it took a year to track down the Yoders up here in Upper Michigan."

The Yoders were an Amish family that had taken over the Maki chicken ranch, which had been stocked with a large number of laying hens that the women's husbands, Toivo and Eino, had won in a poker game. The egg business boomed, enriching all the females involved. The men were left out of the loop.

"What about all the chickens!" Evi said as she picked up a suspicious-looking bottle of wine that was sitting on Tami's doily-covered "tea" table. Evi scowled at the wine. She was used to a box with a spigot.

"Put the bottle down!" snapped Tami. "It has to breathe."

"Whaa?" said Evi, quickly setting the wine back. "What's with the bottle? I mean, the boxed stuff was..."

High On The Vine

"I'll explain, but it's complicated, Tami said. "If you ask me, I think Hannah's hubby, Thomas, didn't like her association with us 'English' or our cookbook deal, and he found an excuse to take her away from the so-called corruption of the modern world."

"Poor Hannah," Evi said. "Now about the wine..."

"Oh, Hannah will be fine, trust me," Tami said. "Sounds like the Amish women know how to get around their menfolk."

"And the chickens and, um, about this wine..." Evi continued.

"I'll get to the wine. Honestly Evi, you are so impatient. The chickens are gone. Good riddance I say."

Except, thought Evi, they made darn good money off the eggs, meat and their *Famish Cooking* cookbook, which combined Finnish and Amish cooking and included a lot of chicken and egg recipes. It had even been featured on the Just Shut up and Eat it! cooking show on Channel 13. Tami and Evi had gotten most of their recipes from Hannah Yoder, and now their source seemed to have vanished. Evi felt a cold knot in her stomach. If the chicken and egg money dried up along with the recipes, she might have to go back to being a flag person for the county road commission. Currently she was on disability, which would run out soon. Perhaps it had not been smart to have called everyone losers when she went into the road commission office to fill out some insurance paperwork. Or to tell her boss to suck an egg.

"The chickens actually went back to the farmer who lost them to Toivo and Eino in that poker game, Tami said. "I convinced Toivo to have a rematch and he may have thrown the game a bit, as per my suggestion."

"So, no chickens?" Evi said.

"Nope, just a lot of, er, chicken residue."

"No egg money?"

"Nope. However, as we all know, when the Good Lord closes one door, He opens another."

Evi had heard this before, but the closing doors seemed to well outnumber those that opened. She looked again at the uncorked wine bottle. How long did the damn thing need to breathe for God's sake? And why were there grapes and cheese and fussy little crackers sitting on Tami's cut-glass plate instead of scones or cookies? What was happening to the Maki women's business "teatime?"

"So," Tami said rubbing her hands together, "remember the monks that rented the place before it became a chicken ranch?"

"Is this stupid wine done breathing?" Evi said.

"Oh, for heaven's sake, go ahead and try it. Tell me what you think."

Evi sloshed some into a goblet and took a guzzle. Sour SOUR **SOUR!** Her face contorted violently while her eyeballs twizzled.

"It's very dry, I'm told," Tami said.

"Drah!" Evi rasped, trying to will her throat to open back up.

"Have a piece of cheese and some grapes," Tami said. "It will refresh your palate."

Evi went for the cheese. She only liked her grapes fermented.

"So, you remember when we had the chicken ranch as a vacation rental we called the Wholey Hideaway and we rented it to a group of monks?" Tami said, reaching for her goblet and pouring a small splash of the wine in it. She sipped then let it play around in her mouth for a while and finally swallowed it (suppressing a grimace) then took a wafer cracker for her palate. "Very fruity and playful."

"Sounds like a gay person," Evi said, trying to swallow one of the cardboard discs that was definitely not baked by the Keebler elves.

High On The Vine

"Evi! Honestly, when will you *please* quit being so, so...disrespectful?"

Evi poured some more of the pucker juice into her goblet. One thing was for certain, a bottle held a whole lot less than a box, which given how slow it was going down was probably a good thing.

"So, *anyway*, we had the group of monks—The Benevolent Brotherhood of Sylvan Monks—rent the place because of what it *didn't* have, such as electricity, WiFi, internet, running water and so on."

"Oh yeah, now I remember," said Evi. "They wouldn't do business with women and they made jams and jellies and sold them to tourists. Wonder if they only sold them to men."

"Well, they could sell things to women, just not cut business deals," Tami said, somewhat exasperated.

"How convenient," Evi said, sniffing her wine, searching for the playfulness.

"ANYWAY," Tami said, "things have changed for the monks—it was inadvertent actually. Apparently, some of their jam/jelly fruit got a little funky and they tried their hand at making wine, and voila! it's a big hit. Trouble is, they need a larger place to run their operation. There isn't adequate room or the right zoning or something at their jam shop."

Evi was all ears. She sensed a reprieve from the road commission flagger job.

"So, as we speak," Tami said, "the Benevolent Brotherhood of Sylvan Monks is out at the former chicken ranch cleaning things up in preparation for the conversion from chicken ranch to winery. It seems that the jam and jelly business has actually been good to them and, having taken a vow of poverty, they must find something to do with all that cash, besides donate it to the needy."

Evi was feeling very needy at the moment. Needing desperately to have some REAL wine, not this toxic brew that they were trying to pass off as anything other than maybe some kind of nasty tonic.

"So, here's the deal," Tami said, taking another tiny sip of the sample wine. Tami had to admit to herself only that the damn stuff was pretty sour. She would, of course, acquire a taste if it killed her.

Evi looked expectantly at Tami. Neither seemed eager to polish off their wine.

"They are fronting all of the money for the conversion, the licensing, even adding a big generator. They will lease the place from us for a dollar a month..."

"Whaaaa!" Evi said, "a dollar?"

"Yes, just as Yoders did. But here's the deal, we get a cut of the profits, just like the Yoders gave us," Tami said.

Evi nibbled on a piece of cheese. She would probably stop and get a personal-size pizza on her way home, as Tami's offerings were definitely below par. "Hannah gave us egg money, which she hid from her husband. Otherwise, I don't think we would have seen a nickel," she said.

"Well, this will be a regular business deal, not under the table," Tami said with an indignant sniff.

"But I thought these monk dudes didn't do 'business' with us inferior women folk," Evi said, eyeing the grapes. She wondered if they had seeds. She had just had some dental work done and didn't need to chomp down on a seed.

"Yes, well, I have already worked that out."

"I don't think we'll get our husbands to help," Evi interrupted. "Eino has been complaining about how you and I took over their hunting camp. They want it back. I don't think they'll be too happy to know that these wine-making monks are the new tenants. Now if they were brewing beer..."

"It's true," Tami said. "I did trick Toivo into losing all those chickens in the rematch perhaps misleading him a bit about getting the camp back. But we don't need our husbands this time. I have a much better idea."

"I'm all ears," Evi said as she took another tiny sip. It may have gone down a little easier.

"Well, now hear me out. See, I told them that you were actually a man, but were one of those LGBT people that didn't know what bathroom you felt comfortable in, so you dressed up like a woman sometimes..."

"What!" shrieked Evi, spraying a fine mist of wine across the room.

"So, you just need to sign the paperwork as Eddie Maki and we have no worries," Tami said with forced cheerfulness. "Then we're living high on the vine!"

Evi thought the expression was "high on the hog," but she got her cousin's drift. She also thought about her options, which were limited. She couldn't rely on Eino, who hadn't worked more than a two-week stretch in his entire life. She could return to the road commission and stand out in the baking sun with that stupid stop/slow sign for ten hours a day while motorists flipped her off and threw garbage at her. Or she could pretend to be a man. She wondered if Eino would even notice. "Okay," she said, "but you have to spring for some leather pants and a new leather jacket that will, um, modify my body profile."

"Deal," Tami said, smiling broadly. "Shall we have a toast?"

The two women (or one woman and one questionable) stared at their goblets, which still held the toxic amber fluid posing as fruit of the vine.

"Let's hit the casino," Tami said. "It's ladies' day!"

Evi gave her a look.

"Oh, right," Tami said. "Well, you don't need to sign the papers until next week, so you're still, er, female or at least gender-neutral."

"You buyin'?"

Tami sighed. This was going to cost her big, she just knew it. "Sure Eddie, my treat."

The Whole Cluster Stomp

Evi took a sip of the latest brew. She thought about the possibility of her very own toe jam being in there, and she gave a small shudder. She wondered what the odds were that she was actually drinking wine made from the grapes she had stomped. In any event, likely *someone's* toe jam was in the mix.

She also wondered when the ever-so-faint-but-still-very-much-there grape stains would finally disappear from her feet. When she last checked, pale bluish tints prevailed along the edge of her toenails and in the ridges of her calloses.

"Stomping grapes adds to the whole profile of the wine," Brother Barnabas, head monk of the Benevolent Brotherhood of Sylvan Monks, had proclaimed. "The resulting mash offers more spice and body to the end product," he added. The grape mash was another whole story along with Evi's requirement to switch to the male gender in order to do business with the monks, who viewed women better suited to whole cluster wine stomping than cutting a business deal.

Evi took another sip of her toe jam wine. Well, she called it that in her mind, but its official name was something like Fruit of the Forest or Fruit of the Finest or Monk Juice, for short. And while it wouldn't win any snooty wine tasting contests, the Monk Juice was selling like pasties at a church fundraiser. They even had a web site and enjoyed a brisk internet business. And though the stuff tasted like pond scum, nobody would admit it. To do so would brand one as a hopeless lowlife and possibly a heretic.

Thrice-removed cousins, Tami & Evi Maki, were having their weekly BEEP meeting, or "teatime." Husbands, Toivo and Eino, had been banished to camp by their wives until possibly spring, or longer if need be. The boys' hunting camp, formerly located where the monk winery operated, was currently wherever the mood took the Maki men. They had acquired a derelict school bus, they called the Blunderbuss, that they moved about at will, so long as they had gas money.

The Maki women's teatime always took place in Tami's "parlor" (living room) and never involved tea. During this particular tealess teatime, the women enjoyed a cozy fire in the woodstove and to a lesser degree, a bottle of Monk Juice, which was being consumed more as a taste test than for pleasure. Tami was determined to be a wine connoisseur and had provided cardboard disc wafers, kiwi fruit and cheese cubes to go along with the Monk Juice. These, she insisted, were the things needed to clear one's palate. For what, Evi wasn't sure, as it would take more than a dry starchy wafer to kill the puckery aftertaste of Monk Juice from one's mouth. Gone were Tami's famous buttery flaky croissants and smoked salmon with dilled cream cheese on bagels and fruit tartlets because they somehow did not "compliment" the wine. Tami did concede that the Forest Fruit/Monk Juice was a bit juvenile and of a delinquent vintage.

"It would appear that our cut of the monthly profits will be in the neighborhood of $2,000," Tami said to Evi, who nearly choked on the bone-dry wafer that she was trying to swallow.

"That's $1,000 each!" Evi shrieked, spewing a few wafer crumbs across the tea table. This was good news indeed because her disability checks were stopping in exactly 17 days at which time she would have to either fish or cut bait;

quit or go back to her job as the slow/stop construction sign-turner with the county road commission, a prospect that kept her awake at night. $1,000 a month would nicely fill the gap once the disability checks stopped.

"Of course, that's pre-tax," Tami added.

Tax, smax. She and Eino never worried too much about filing tax returns.

In spite of some minor inconveniences, such as having to pose as "Eddie" in order to do business with the misogynistic monks, the wine-making business was the best scheme that she and Tami had jumped into. While the erstwhile chicken/egg business did have its benefits, it seemed that bookkeeping with the Amish Yoder clan who managed the Maki chicken ranch was a bit loose. Evi had always suspected that she and Tami hadn't received their fair share of the egg money. Beneath all that propriety, the Amish could be very shrewd.

"And we are getting *slammed* with Christmas orders," Tami said as she took a very tiny sip from her wine glass, suppressing a grimace. "According to Brother Barnabas, the Pinot Gristly should be aged a full six months by next week and we can put it on the market. The White Infidel will be shortly after. It's a bit cloudy right now and needs to settle."

Evi poured a little more Monk Juice into her goblet. This particular batch was supposed to be something called Red Rosary. She noted a grape seed spiraling downward in the nectar. There had been some talk about difficulties with proper filtering after the Whole Cluster Stomp. The term "whole cluster" refers to a bunch of grapes, still on the stems and likely smattered with bird droppings and general atmospheric toxins that supposedly disappear during fermentation. Some wine makers use a machine to de-stem and crush the grapes. Very pricey. The Benevolent Brotherhood of Sylvan Monks decided that they could forego having to make the purchase and get people to come stomp the juice out of the grapes, called maceration, not only for free, but for a fee! Plus, they insisted, the stems added texture to the brew, which was like saying that gristle added character to a steak.

While Evi was still learning about wine making, she was pretty sure that all the wine she had consumed prior to the Benevolent Brotherhood of Sylvan Monk winery venture was largely free of debris, except maybe a little backflush.

"The grape stomp was a great idea!" Tami enthused. "Brother Barnabas, in spite of his vow of poverty, has a good head for business. Imagine people *paying* to have fun crushing the grapes! Brilliant!"

"I didn't see any of the monks slogging around in that sludge," Evi said. She had gotten a Charlie horse in her hip from all the stomping, which was far more work than fun. Evi popped a cheese cube into her mouth and hoped its binding ability would offset the galloping trots that the Monk Juice inevitably triggered.

"Well, no of course, they had to collect the product and properly handle it for the next stage," Tami said, running her tongue over her teeth. A tiny piece of something woody had lodged itself between her teeth. She sucked at it and set it free. Loath to swallow the unknown, Tami discretely deposited it in a napkin and gave it a brief inspection. A piece of stem.

"And Toivo and Eino were no help," Evi groused.

Toivo and Eino had been browbeaten by their wives to attend the Whole Cluster Stomp in order to lend a male element. While Evi cum Eddie was the male representative during business dealings with the monks, she converted back to her God-assigned gender during the Stomp. Several monks had noted a familiarity between Eddie and Evi who explained that they were closely related, which was not a lie.

The Whole Cluster Stomp

Though the tourists did a lot of the grape stomping—and paid handsomely for the privilege—Toivo and Eino were to pair up with their wives to stomp a batch of bunches in a sizable lager, which was actually the cement water trough left over from the Yoders who used it to water their livestock. The drain plug had a makeshift spigot attached for the juice to flow out of.

Dozens of couples, somewhat tipsy from a visit to the tasting room, enthusiastically tromped away in their individual vats of grapes. Energetic accordion music played a lively polka, encouraging stompers to keep up the rhythm. Monks dashed about, catching the pulpy juice that spewed from little spigots attached to the vats. When it was time for the Makis to strip off shoes and socks, Toivo and Eino were nowhere to be found, though it wasn't hard to figure out where they had snuck off to.

"Someone had to oversee the tasting room," Tami had pointed out.

"Wolf guarding the sheep," Evi muttered.

And Tami had declared that she was coming down with a virus at the time of the stomp, so left Evi to mash several bushels of grapes on her own. The process held all the appeal of wallowing in a bog full of slimy eels.

"The Whole Custer Stomp will be an annual event, I'm sure," Tami said. "We'll make it a festival and really do it up next year. We'll get Channel 13 to come and do a story!"

Given the track record of the Maki women's business dealings and the fact that the wine product was not exactly top shelf, Evi wondered if Monk Juice would just be another fleeting scheme and that she would be groveling for her old job back at the road commission as the slow/stop construction sign turner.

"You will need to convert to your Eddie persona and talk to Brother Barnabas about the slurry dumped out behind the fermentation building," Tami said to Evi. "I'm afraid that little incident has gotten the health inspector sniffing around."

The "incident" to which Tami referred involved the girls' husbands who would find trouble in a vacuum.

"Being a religious enterprise there is a question of jurisdiction. Whether we're cited or not, I do declare the odor *still* lingers large. It wafted into the tasting room at the most inopportune moment and disrupted the experience of our paying customers. I never saw a room clear so quickly in my life, and that includes last Thanksgiving when Toivo ate some bad oyster stuffing."

"I don't like being Eddie," Evi whined. "I mean, I don't mind wearing the getup, but I can't ever use a public restroom. And I REFUSE to go out back like those two cretins we're married to. I mean, why do men do that. What is so 'manly' about going around behind a building and…"

"I'm well aware what Toivo and Eino did, and now they are dearly paying the price," Tami snapped. "Until the odor wears off, Toivo will not be coming into my house."

"I had to burn Eino's clothes, and it still didn't kill the schmell," Evi added, her tongue feeling a little thick.

"I think every animal in the forest was at that slurry pile getting inebriated on fermented waste," Tami said.

"Until the skunk family came. Then all the schmart crittersh sheedaddled," Evi said. She found that if she took a sip of Monk Juice then added the slippery kiwi fruit, it made things interesting."

"Like you said," Tami quipped, "The *smart* ones left. Then there was Toivo and Eino."

"Not shhooo schmart," Evi said. She wondered if kiwi did something to enhance the alcohol content. Maybe "Eddie" should talk to Brother Barnabas about kiwi wine. She had to admit that while the Monk Juice tasted vile, it packed a punch and she felt like she'd gone ten rounds.

The Whole Cluster Stomp

"Well, they'll have a good long time in the Blunderbuss to enjoy one another's company," Tami said.

"You shaaad it shitsir!" Evi slurred. She found it weird, but her tongue seemed to have fallen asleep, with the rest of her following suit.

Tami tutted as she covered her snoring cousin with an Afghan. Some Maki! Cousin Evi never could hold her liquor.

Setting Up Shoppe

"I do think that the Burgundy Chocolate Walnut Supreme fudge is my best effort," Tami said to Evi.

Tami and Evi Maki were having their weekly BEEP meeting in Tami's parlor. As usual, there was no tea present, but rather an open bottle of wine—labeled Burgundy Blessing—and a plate of fudge. Absent was the ghastly plate of palate-cleansing cardboard wafers and bland cubes of cheese generally present at these wine-tasting meetings.

The two women had engaged in numerous entrepreneurial ventures over the past few years, the current being a co-ownership in a winery run by the Benevolent Brotherhood of Sylvan Monks, a misogynous group of brothers who admitted there had been a learning curve with wine making. The product, branded as "Monk Juice," was not so much playful but more aptly described as immature if not downright infantile. Like a wayward child, Monk Juice had some growing up to do.

"It all works for me!" Evi said as she plucked a piece of fudge off the nicely arranged crystal plate sitting on the "tea" table. She alternated sipping (and grimacing) wine and devouring a piece of fudge, which served as a kind of chaser. "You do make a mean batch of fudge," Evi said.

"It's selling well at the winery," Tami said. Generally,

High On The Vine

Tami did not abide bragging, except when it was true, such as this was, in which case it was merely stating a fact. "I'm glad I came up with the idea. Who would have thought fudge and wine would go so well together? I did have a bit of trouble getting the fudge to set up after adding wine to it, but the marshmallow cream did the trick." What Tami didn't mention was that she actually only added cooking wine to the fudge, as the Monk Juice ended up compromising it to the point of unpalatability. When she listed the ingredients on the package as including "wine" it wasn't her fault that the assumption may be made that it was Monk Juice rather than something imported from California that she picked up at the IGA.

Evi found that as time went on and more Monk Juice was consumed, it began to—if not improve—at least trigger less gagging. She took another piece of the Burgundy Chocolate Walnut Supreme fudge. No trouble getting it down! She briefly thought of her annoying doctor who warned her about her pre-diabetes and gave stern instructions to eliminate sugar and carbs in her diet. "Lots of fruit and vegetables!" Doctor Nitpik had said. Well, wine's main ingredient was fruit, wasn't it?

"So, this has given me a wonderful idea!" Tami said.

Evi wasn't sure how many more of Tami's wonderful ideas she could afford, with her charge card hovering around its limit. But since her disability had run out with the road commission, and she opted to NEVER go back to her former job there as the token female slow/stop construction zone sign-turner, she was hopelessly hitched to Tami's wagon. Her spouse, Eino, had not held a steady job since—ever. Evi took another sip of Monk Juice to brace herself for her cousin's latest "wonderful idea."

Tami took a dainty sip of her wine, shuttered a bit, then squared her shoulders. "There's a nice little shop—well former shop—in town for rent."

"Uh huh," Evi said, pouring the last of the Burgundy Blessing into her wine goblet.

"If we sign a two-year lease, we get 90 days rent-free," Tami continued.

"Uh huh, Evi said as she got up to retrieve another bottle from the kitchen. "I'm listening," she muttered.

"Then it's very reasonable after that," Tami said.

"Uh huh," Evi said from the kitchen where she wrestled with getting the cork out of the stupid bottle. Why in heck couldn't those blasted monks put wine in a box where it belonged—with a spigot? Evi longed for the simplicity of wine consumption in the Maki women's earlier meetings.

"We could call it, oh I don't know, T&E Wine and Fudge Shoppe," Tami said. "You know, spell shop S-H-O-P-P-E, like Ye Olde."

Evi returned to the parlor with the new bottle of wine. This one was called Crown of Thorns Brambleberry. She had accidentally broken off the cork, and several chunks were floating in the brew. Maybe it would improve the flavor. Evi had no idea what fudge would go with Crown of Thorns Brambleberry and she didn't give a wit. So far she hadn't met a fudge she didn't like. "Teepee Ye Olde Wine and Fudge Shoppe?" she said, setting the bottle on the table. "Sorry about the cork. Teepee? Is the shop, like, a teepee or something?"

"Not teepee. T&E, for Tami and Evi. Not Ye Olde—just plain old Shoppe."

"Teepee Plain Ol' Wine and Fudge Ssshop?" Evi said. She noticed her tongue seemed to be a little numb.

"No, you ninny—oh never mind," Tami said. "We can figure that out later. Anyway, we can also have things of local interest besides fudge and wine. You know, products from local artists. Honey, maple syrup, crafts and other touristy stuff."

"Uh huh," Evi said, eyeing the last piece of fudge. "Do we have more fudge?"

"No," Tami snapped. "We have to watch our profit-margin."

"I didn't know you put margarine in the fudge. Why ish we watshing it? Ish there a margarine ssshortage?" Evi said. Her tongue had definitely lost all feeling.

"As a matter of fact, I do put—oh for heaven's sake! Why are we talking about fudge ingredients?" Tami said snippily.

"Wahl don't get mad at me," Evi said. "Yoush brought it up!" she added, taking another swallow from her goblet. The thorny bramble stuff wasn't too bad. Similar to Mercy Merlot, but with more of a poke—or even a stab.

"ANYWAY," Tami said, we need to sign the lease IMMEDIATELY before some cannabis shop or other ridiculous thing goes in there. And, well, it seems that my wonderful husband, Toivo, has sullied our credit to the point that our score is, shall we say, below par. I need you to be the signer."

"Singer? Yous know I canna shhhing," Evi said. She found that the last piece of Burgundy Chocolate whatever fudge went just fine with the Thorny Thing wine.

"Sign-er!" Tami said. "I need you to SIGN the lease."

"Shuuur," no prob." Evi felt a little woozy. Probably her blood sugar. She remembered the doctor's instructions, so consumed some more liquid fruit.

"And I've already talked to local artisans who will place their arts and crafts in our store," Tami said. "I, of course, plan to have my tatted doilies prominently displayed."

"Uh, huh," Evi said, her eyes drooping. Then she suddenly perked up. "Hey, what about Eino's fungush shhculptureesh?"

"Well..." Tami said, trying to imagine a fungus sculpture as anything but disgusting.

"He takessh them to the gun shows and shhells them to the peeps there. Once he figured out how to varnish 'em so they don't shhtink, they shhhell like hahcakes!"

Tami ignored her cousin, who simply could not hold her spirits. It was a disgrace to the Maki name. Fungus! Hardly upscale.

"He tried making clockssshh too, outta chunks of wood, but didna work sssho hot. Ushhing it assshhh a door shhtop. Workshh good."

Tami realized that to have Evi sign the contract while inebriated was an excellent idea. She was glad she had the document tucked in her nearby purse. She would be the first to admit that the "shop" would need a bit of fixing up. It had been a shoe repair shop in its previous life, and the smell of ancient leather and shoe dye had hung heavily in the air when Tami had toured the place with the overly-eager real estate agent, Martha, who was managing the property.

"Just look at that view!" Martha had enthused as she waved her arm toward the grimy front window that basically had a view of the street and unfortunately sported a full-length crack that was repaired with a long strip of duct tape. "And the location!" she continued. "The tourists will positively flock in during the summer. A little paint and some elbow grease, and you've got a heck of a sweet place here!"

Tami had frowned at the cracked and peeling linoleum, which the agent noticed.

"They are doing wonders with planked flooring these days. I think it's on sale right now at the Kangas You-Do-It Emporium. And I think paint is too. AND I happen to have a nice selection of display fixtures in my, er, garage that I am practically giving away."

Tami made a non-committal noise and looked up at the crumbling plaster ceiling.

"No problem with leaks up there," Martha said. "I mean, there's an apartment above here—a very nice, er, young couple rent it. And if there's a roof leak, it has a long way to go before it comes down here. Hee hee!"

"How much?" Tami said.

"Well, it is a prime commercial spot," the agent had said.

"Uh huh," Tami said.

"I can let you have it as a steal for a thousand a month!"

Tami looked at the agent and wondered for the first time if she was high on something. The agent sensed the deal slipping away.

"Okay, five hundred..."

Tami engaged in a study of her fingernails. She could practically feel the agent squirm. Ridiculous! They should pay her to take over the place.

"There is someone else looking at..." the agent began.

"A hundred bucks a month, with no rent for the first three months, plus half of the cost of repairs and fixing this dump up," Tami said.

The agent's mouth almost hit the floor.

"And you can throw in those so-called fixtures that probably need to go to the recycle center," Tami added.

"Well I..."

"This little shop of horrors should be condemned. I'm afraid to even look at the bathroom," Tami said.

"I'd need a two-year lease," said the agent.

"Deal."

"Wonderful! I'll just do a credit check and draw up the lease this afternoon."

***

Tami looked at her sacked-out cousin, who somehow had salvaged her credit score, in spite of her less than credible husband, Eino. It was very simple, Agent Martha had said. Tami just needed a co-signer with an acceptable credit score and the deal was sealed. Tami went to the kitchen and pulled out a piece of Maple Chardonnay Smoothie Cream fudge from a container she had hidden in the laundry cupboard. She grabbed the lease document and a pen from her purse and returned to the parlor where Evi was snoring softly. Tami stooped over her cousin and waved the fudge under her nose to arouse her.

Worked like a charm.

Getting Your Wickiup

"I do believe that the faux animal skin canopy lends itself well to the store theme," Tami said to Evi. "It gives the place a rustic appearance of the Northwoods, don't you think?"

The Maki women were sitting in their new entrepreneurial endeavor, The Wickiup Wine and Fudge Shoppe, a tourist trap shop that would undoubtedly lead to wealth and early retirement. Though making a blocky, cramped retail space that was formerly a shoe repair shop into anything thematic had its challenges.

Evi nodded. She wasn't about to tell her "politically correct" cousin that some of the animal skins were not so-called "faux." Evi's husband, Eino, donated them from his "war chest," which was a smelly trunk in the attic full of man stuff. Some of the pelts were booty from poker games. Some were from roadkill. None had actually been skillfully hunted for food or sport by either Eino or his cousin, Toivo. The Maki family tree was more tangled than a tag alder thicket since the whole batch were cousins to some degree or other and the guys were uncles to boot. This made for a mini family reunion when the four of them got together, which was usually only by accident.

"And the nature sounds certainly add to the ambiance," Tami continued, closing her eyes as if meditating while she swayed slightly to the sound of a waterfall being broadcast throughout the store—a sound that made Evi need to use the restroom.

"I'm so glad I got the technology figured out so I could download a playlist of the sounds of woods, water and wildlife," Tami said.

It actually had been Evi who had figured out how to work the quirky ins and outs of the musical technology. But it wasn't only waterfalls, thunderstorms, yipping coyotes, and loon calls that played. There was also annoying Native American pipe music that Evi was certain would drive customers away never to return. The only way to distract customers from the eerie warbling was to load them up with a couple of Monk Juice samples. Monk Juice was actually a rustic local wine whose production was sponsored by the Maki women. As far as Evi was concerned, the freebies were getting out of hand and probably were cutting into the bottom line. She herself of course was entitled to periodically sample everything edible and drinkable, as a kind of quality control inspector.

"What do you think about putting up some birch bark wallpaper?" Tami said. "I know we threw a coat of paint on the walls before we opened this place, but it seems so—ordinary. Not like a wickiup when you get inside. Also, I think we should circulate some pine scent throughout. It smells rather musty, in spite of the mold removal we made the landlord perform."

Evi had to admit that the décor was bland and it smelled like a dozen cats had lived there without the benefit of a litter box. However, rather than smelling like a pungent car air freshener, Evi suggested wafting the cooking fudge aroma throughout and even venting it into the street would be more of a draw. They did that in the fudge shops on Mackinac Island.

"Well," Tami had said in response to Evi's suggestion, "perhaps a little sniff of my Peanut Butter Pinot Creamy

Delight would be irresistible. I had actually been thinking of that myself." Tami had a way of always taking credit for Evi's ideas and Evi had a way of always paying for Tami's. However, Tami was an accomplished confectioner whose talents had long been appreciated by Evi who let the things like stealing one's idea slide. Besides, the fudge was now a lucrative tourist attraction. They secretly called these tourists "fudgies."

"Bark wallpaper? Real bark?" Evi said, moving over to the wine display. Today's Monk Juice was Resurrection Red Rosé. It was disturbingly bright red. They called it Res Red for sort, as the word resurrection often became difficult to pronounce after a few ounces of sampling.

"Oh, it would be a vinyl printed wallpaper," Tami said. "I've got a decorator coming later. Also, maybe some window treatments that simulate whatever it is they used in wickiup windows." Tami got out her phone and began tapping on the screen. "I'm Gaggling wickiup windows," she said. "Hmm. I'm not getting anything, though there is a nice resort in Utah called Wicked Widows."

"Maybe it's 'cause there are no windows in wickiups," Evi said.

"Don't be silly. Whoever heard of no windows?" Tami said.

Evi shrugged. "I guess they might have grass shades like on Gilligan's Island, or maybe more animal skins," she said, as she began driving a corkscrew into the Res Red. Every time she had to open one of the infernal bottles of Monk Juice, she longed for the chicken ranch days of boxed wine with the handy spigot that she and Tami shared. Corks were almost as obstinate as her husband Eino.

Tami looked up at the crumbling, water-stained ceiling. "I'm thinking wood supports up here—simulated limbs and branches, you know, to carry on the wickiup motif."

High On The Vine

Evi wondered where the heck you'd find simulated tree parts. Probably on e-Pay or something. How many people would even look up and notice?

Chicken ranch notwithstanding, Evi Maki had to admit that Tami had gotten them into a good one this time. Originally, Evi had thought it was a mistake to give up the chicken ranching business and take up wine making with The Sylvan Benevolent Bunch of Misogynistic Monks. However, having the Wickiup Wine and Fudge Shoppe was something she could sink her teeth into. Literally. Not only was there her cousin's delicious fudge, but also all other kinds of touristy snacks, like saltwater taffy (which didn't taste salty at all), peanut brittle, moose munch, ice cream, Moon Pies, Little Debbie snack cakes, sub sandwiches, pork rinds—you name it. All of it forbidden by her persnickety doctor because of her so-called pre-diabetes. So long as she consumed fruit and vegetables along with an occasional sweet treat, she was golden. This was where the generous consumption of Monk Juice came into her food pyramid since it was 100% pure (though somewhat adulterated) fruit. It was also a good seller in the Wickiup Shoppe. And at grape harvest time, it provided a tourist attraction with the Annual Wine Stomping Jamboree out at the winery.

The Wickiup also had a wide assortment of local products, such as Maple syrup and honey, along with a selection of regional books and crafty stuff from the area artisans. Evi was quite proud of the looks her hubby's "Fun with Fungus" masterpieces got from the tourists who filed through the shop, sipping their Dixie Cups of Monk Juice and nibbling on a sample of the fudge of the day. In a way, she was amazed that people would actually hand over their plastic debit cards to buy something that Eino had hacked off a rotting log in the woods and sealed with a coat of cheap varnish. Laminated animal turds were Eino's next project, once he could find a laminator to use. The library refused him theirs on the grounds that he was an idiot.

The name of the Maki cousins' little store was supposed to be T&E Wine and Fudge Shoppe. Somehow Evi thought Tami said *teepee* instead of T&E—probably something to do with her blood sugar being too high or too low. Given that they were actually very near the Ojibwa Indian Reservation, Tami had allowed that tying into the Native American theme was, as she said, "prudent." However, since the Ojibwa Indians never actually had teepees, but rather wigwams or wickiups, Tami suggested they be politically correct and go with wickiup.

Evi finally managed to get the cork out of the Res Red and place it on the freebie table, along with various tiny cubes of fudge with little toothpicks sticking out of them. She barely had time to flip the sign in the door from "closed" to "open" when a burly man barged in, setting off the little tinkle of the bell installed over the door to alert the Maki women of customer comings and goings.

"Welcome to the Wickiup Wine and Fud..." Tami began.

"What the..." snarled the burly man.

"Just browsing or can we help you find something?" Tami said. "Today's Monk Juice is..."

"Monk *what*?" said the burly man.

"Er, Juice," Tami said. "Wine."

"Yea, yea," said the man. "Where's Buck?"

"I beg your pardon?" Tami said.

"The owner—you know, the dude who, ah, did *business*?"

"You mean the shoe repair gentleman?"

"Yea, sure. That's him—shoe repair-hah!" he said and snorted.

"Well, I'm afraid he left some time ago?" Tami said.

"That so?"

High On The Vine

Suddenly the hairs on the back of Tami's neck stood up. It was like the feeling she got when she had a close call with a mama bear in the Thimbleberry patch.

"Er—yes, we are renting..." Tami began.

"Don't give me no crap! I know you broads are just a cover for the jerk," said the man. "Buck owes me my cut—fifty-fifty, and I ain't leavin' till I get it. So hand it over lady."

"Now see here..." Tami began.

"No, missy, you see here. I know this here is a front for Buck's backroom business. Don't play dumb with me."

"I—"

As if on a mystical cue, something from the playlist kicked in, only instead of Native American whistle music, they had a raucous Ojibwa drumming/singing pow wow number blast over the sound system, causing everyone to jump two feet in the air.

"What th..." said the burly man who pulled a gun out of his belt and shot a hole in the ceiling. An avalanche of plaster came down on him, turning him into a burly ghost. Tami and Evi hit the deck from the fear of plaster and bullets.

Just then, the minibus from the Gnarly Woods Senior Complex pulled up and a stream of senior citizens poured into the shop. The singers/drummers pow wow number continued to blare away. The burly man was trying to get the plaster dust out of his eyes and accidentally dropped his gun.

"Hey!" said an old lady from the senior group. "Is this here one of them enactments—like a stickup?"

"Myrtle! Get away from that man," barked a frizzy red headed woman.

"Wanna take me hostage?" the Myrtle woman said.

"You're all crazy!" shouted the now gun-less burly man. "Get away from me you old bag!"

"Who are you calling an old bag?" snapped the Myrtle woman, picking up the man's gun. "I had me one of these 'til they took it away after I shot my husband. He cheated on me."

Everyone hit the deck again, including all the seniors— except an old man on a scooter who cranked up his motor and rammed into the burly man.

"Oooff! Get. Away. From. Me. You. Old. Fart."

"Old fart, eh?" said scooter man as he ran over the burly man's foot.

"Ahhhh!

Tami picked up the phone and called 9-1-1.

"She's callin' the fuzz!" shrieked Myrtle still waving the gun around. "Hot diggidy dog!"

"Tell Buck this ain't over!" said the burly plaster-crusted man as he limped toward the door. "I think that old geezer broke my foot! You'll hear from my..."

"Git!" said Myrtle, waving the gun menacingly.

The man got out just before she put a round in the door.

Everyone was deaf for a moment, ears ringing from the gunshot. The drumming/singing mercifully thudded to an end. Once their hearing returned, folks heard the distinct wail of sirens approaching.

"So," said Myrtle blowing on the barrel of the gun. "How about some of that booze yous are givin' out?"

"Certainly," said Tami. "Although we'd appreciate it if you would perhaps put the weapon down."

"Yea. Good idea before the cops get here," she said.

Evi was wondering how to explain things to the police when they arrived. Many of them—well all of them—were not all that fond of the Makis in general, and Evi had no idea what had just happened. She was feeling a little woozy and figured that her blood sugar was on the fritz, so headed for some fruit refreshment. One thing she did know, she was going to find out more about the Wicked Widow Resort that her cousin had found online. It was time for a break.

Cash Flow Problems

"I swear that we were being followed," Tami said to Evi. The two Maki cousins were heading toward the wine tasting area inside their latest entrepreneurial venture: The Wickiup Wine and Fudge Shoppe, a tourist trap if there ever was one. Tami and Evi had proven to be good hunters of tourists and especially enjoyed the success of their locally manufactured wine: Monk Juice.

"Ya think it has anything to do with that burly guy who came in here looking for whatsisname who used to rent this place before us? Evi said. "What was his name?"

"Chuck or Buck—I don't know," Tami said. "When that burly guy was waving a gun around, I naturally wasn't paying a lot of attention to who he was looking for. Anyway, I've seen that car following us before. I'm sure because, after all, there aren't too many black Beemers around here."

"Uh huh," Evi said. "Most everyone drives a truck. What's a Beemer?"

"B-M-W—they call it a Beemer," Tami said. "At least the rich and famous do, because I seriously doubt anyone in our neck of the woods has one of those babies parked in their detached garage. ANYWAY, I imagine the Beemer occupants aren't really following us, but more likely are looking for one of our less than scrupulous husbands over a gambling debt or some shady deal," Tami said.

"Where are the guys, anyway?" Evi said.

"Something about taking the Blunderbuss to a new hunting spot. Of course, there is nothing in season right now except deer flies and ticks. Just an excuse to sit around and drink beer."

Evi went over to the wine cooler and extracted a bottle of chilled super-fruity Sacred Sangria, which was the "juice" of the day. They headed toward one of the small bistro tables they had purchased with part of their winnings from a recent road rally race. The tables were tucked into a cozy back corner of the Wickiup Shoppe, designed to create the proper ambiance for those wishing to enjoy a free sample or two of wine and fudge. Because the Wickiup Shoppe did not have a proper license to *sell* wine by the glass, they simply gave it away finding that this generally resulted in substantial purchases, often by the case, of the unusual and barely palatable Monk Juice.

For some reason Evi was always in charge of the free sample "nook" of the Wickiup Shoppe, which required her to wrestle the stubborn corks out of the wine bottles. In less-pretentious days, Tami and Evi had simply snapped open the spigot of a boxed wine and sat around the woodstove in Tami's parlor (living room) having tea (wine) and contemplating where they had gone wrong in their lives. For example, Tami had once had a government job and Evi had worked for the county road commission, driving a snowplow then later endlessly flipping the slow/stop sign at road construction projects. Today, while it seemed that the two Maki women had come a long way, Evi did long for the boxed-wine days. Not only were they easier to open, but the product was sooooo much tastier.

"So, where are we with our upgrades?" Tami said taking a tiny sip of the Sacred Sangria and sucking in her cheeks a bit before swallowing.

"Well, the soft-serve ice cream machine should be here at the end of the week. I'm looking forward to that!" Evi said. "It supposedly can swirl vanilla AND chocolate into one yummy frozen treat."

"There it goes!" Tami said, jumping up from the table.

"What?" Evi said, giving the corkscrew another vicious twist. "The soft-serve machine?"

"No, dummy, the Beemer. Real slow, it just glided past!"

"Uh huh. Dang!" Evi said. She had managed to break the cork, and was now trying to get the corkscrew into the piece eluding her in the neck in the bottle, without pushing it all the way in.

"It's coming back!"

"What?"

"The Beemer. It's stopping. Get the gun!"

"What?"

"The gun. It's locked in the supply closet. Toivo gave it to me for protection."

Evi abandoned the half-opened bottle of Monk Juice and hustled to the supply closet. "It's locked! Where's the key?"

"Behind the counter, in the..." Tami began.

The front door burst open and two women sauntered in, looking around as if they owned the place. They both had on sunglasses and their eyes obviously hadn't adjusted to the dimmer light, as one, with purple hair and ripped jeans, bumped into a shot glass and coffee mug display, sending several pieces smashing to the ground. The other one, who was blond with black roots and wore colorful stretch pants, was apparently alarmed by the noise and began frantically rummaging through her purse, presumably *not* for her lipstick.

High On The Vine

"You dope," said purple hair, rubbing her shin where she had smacked it on the corner of a display rack. "You should have had your gun ready..."

Evi began a more aggressive search for the key once she heard the word gun.

"Here!" Tami said to Evi as she handed a ring of keys to her cousin.

"I tol' you that damn purse was too big," said purple hair.

"Yea? Well—here it is," said black roots, pulling out a glasses case and pointing it at Tami. "Ooops, my bad."

Tami attempted to distract the bumbling hoodettes while Evi scurried to the supply closet and fumbled with the lock.

"So, ladies, can I help you find anything?" Tami said, trying to hide the quaver in her voice. She well knew there was nothing more dangerous than a bumbling hoodette with a gun. Better off to have a pro who only *intentionally* shoots people.

"Sure can," said purple hair. "You can tell us where the heck Chuck got to!"

"Buck," said black roots. "He's the one who run off with all the loot. Chuck was just his idiot minion."

"Right—Buck."

"Buck?" Tami said. "I'm terribly sorry, but I don't know any Buck—except Bucky Heinkkinnen, who is in the old folks' home."

"Which key is it?" shouted Evi from the supply closet door where she fumbled with the keyring.

"It says Master!" Tami said. "So sorry ladies, my partner was just getting into the, er, supply room to get some more, um free stuff. Would you like to sample...?"

"Can it, sister. Y'all need to start remembering Chuck..."

"Buck!" said black roots.

"Right, whatever, you—oh heck, now I forget what I was supposed to say," said purple hair.

"Found my gun!" said black roots.

"Got it!" yelled Evi, who began rummaging around inside the storage closet.

"Today's Monk Juice is Sanctuary Sangria and our fudge is Sea Salt Caramel," Tami said.

"Monk what?" said black roots. "Anyhow, start singin' or I'll bug you."

"I really don't sing well...Evi, how's it going?"

"Plug—not bug," said purple hair. "Don't you remember anything burly guy taught you?"

Black roots began to snivel just as Evi emerged from the closet brandishing an object. "It's darker than all get-out in there. Is this it?" she yelled.

"No, you dingbat. That's a mop!" Tami yelled.

Evi disappeared back into the closet while black roots opened the chamber on a small handgun. "I think I forgot the bullets," she said.

A loud explosion filled the store, sending a row of commemorative plates of the Bishop Baraga Shrine off their shelf and crashing one by one onto the floor. Purple hair, black roots and Tami dove for cover.

Evi emerged from the supply closet, carrying a shotgun. "So, what did Toivo load this thing for, anyway?" she asked. "Bigfoot?"

Tami peeked over the counter and watched the hoodettes crawl for the exit.

"Hey, I'm not paid enough for this crap," said black roots. "I'm going back to my old job at the Purple Fox."

"Are they looking for another pole dancer?" asked purple hair.

The bell over the door tinkled as the two hoodettes slunk out. Tami could see Burly Guy standing by the Beemer, intensely scowling.

"Come back again!" Tami said, her voice dripping with sarcasm.

"Bite me!" said black roots over her shoulder as the two scurried to the Beemer and shoved Burly Guy behind the wheel then dove in the back seat and sped off.

"Um, Tami, you might outta come look at something," Evi said.

Tami sighed and followed her cousin. The two picked their way through some scattered debris created by the shotgun blast. Tami was actually quite amazed she hadn't heard any sirens. Good thing the upstairs tenants were gone all day. She wondered if there was any damage in their apartment. From what she heard about their housekeeping habits it would be unlikely they'd notice.

"So, what kind of mess—holy cow!" Tami shrieked.

"Yea, I mean wowzer, right?" Evi said.

A substantial pile of cash had settled on the floor of the closet, while additional bills continued to drift whimsically down from a hole in the ceiling.

"Musta been, like, a secret compartment or something where the cash was stashed," Evi said.

Tami simply stood with her mouth hanging open and uttering a prayer of thanks that, indeed, no sirens could be heard. The disposition of this newfound munificence from above would need a good "think."

"So, I'm guessing that this is what Burly Guy and the two hoodettes were talking about?" Evi said.

"I guess Buck or Chuck or whatever his name is wasn't really a shoe repair person," Tami said.

"How much do you think?" Evi said.

"Oodles," Tami said.

"Major oodles," Evi said.

They backed out and shut the door. Tami went to the front door, shut and locked it, and pulled down the "Closed, Please Call Again" shade.

The two cousins went back and peeked into the closet again. The bills had quit falling, though some appeared to be stuck at a trap door that was hanging from one hinge. Tami shut the closet door, grabbed the almost open bottle of wine and plunked down at a table. Evi joined her.

"So," Evi said, pushing the annoying leftover cork piece down into the body of the bottle. She poured each of them a large goblet of wine complete with a few cork floaties.

"So," Tami said, shoving a plate of fudge between them.

The two wrestled briefly with the moral dilemma before them—the money, that is, not the fudge.

"I'm wondering—you know, just asking—where the nearest one of those Beemer dealers is," Evi said.

"Far, far away," Tami said, taking the largest swig of wine in her life, ever. "In Never, Neverland."

"I like a truck better anyhow," Evi said. "Give me a good Yooper truck any day."

Tami polished off her wine then took out her cell phone and sighed. "Hello, 9-1-1, I'd like to report some found property," she said. "What? No, nobody's hurt but you'd better bring a Brinks armored truck."

Women of the
World Warriors
(or not)

"So, tell me again about the getaway," Evi said to Tami as the two women engaged in their weekly Business Enhancement Entrepreneurial Plan (BEEP) meeting. The two Maki cousins were sitting at one of the bistro tables in their latest venture: The Wickiup Wine and Fudge Shoppe. BEEP discussion was a euphemism for drinking wine, or Monk Juice as it was marketed, and nibbling Tami's latest fudge recipe: Double Bean Delight—the beans being vanilla and cocoa, not kidney or garbanzo as might come to mind. The accompanying Monk Juice, a rather murky yellowish concoction, was dubbed: "He is Riesling."

The products in the shop, a bona fide tourist trap situated in their hometown of Budworm featured the Monk Juice, fudge and an assortment of authentic Yooper crafted items such as varnished fungus door stops, along with cheesy "made in China, Taiwan, Shri Lanka and Outer Mongolia" shot glasses, coffee mugs, commemorative plates, tee shirts, hats, fake Native American jewelry and so on. They also sold authentic Lake Superior pebbles by the pound. People

125

actually *paid* for rocks, albeit nice shiny ones. The Wickiup also featured many tasty treats, including a soft-serve ice cream contraption and ICEY drink machine that dispensed a cup shaved ice with a squirt of blue, orange, or red high fructose syrup and sold for $3.00.

"It's not really a getaway, per se," Tami said, as she took a tiny sip of her He is Riesling wine. She had learned to control the instinct to shudder when sipping the Monk Juice, though it took a *lot* of control. Tami's piece of double-bean fudge sat untouched, while Evi had managed to consume three of the neat little squares. In Evi's option, mixing vanilla and chocolate was pure genius.

"If it were simply a vacation, we would not be able to write it off as a business expense," Tami explained to her rather slow-on-the-take cousin. "Therefore, the organizers have wisely labeled it as: Exclusionary Infusion of Entrepreneurial Inclusive Organization of the Women of the World Warriors. Or: E- I- E- I- O, W-O-W-W."

"Huh?" Evi said, as she reached for another perfect little square of double bean fudge. "Eee, I, Eee I wha?"

"I think they call it WOWW for short," sniffed Tami. "Women only. Whatever it is, it's *not* a luxury getaway disguised as a business trip, which is what men always do. Meeting at golf resorts in tropical places with free booze and shrimp buffets not to mention all those women in skimpy outfits giving them so-called health massages and whatnot. This is a real opportunity!"

"Uh huh," Evi said, refilling her wine goblet. She wouldn't mind a massage and perhaps some real wine and not the vile concoction that the monks produced.

Tami said: "It says on the web site: 'A chance for women of strength to ply their skills and plow through the debris of a man's world'."

Women of the World Warriors (or not)

"Debris?" Evi said. "Where is this? Vegas? Chicago? Hawaii!"

"Funny, they don't say," Tami said. "It does say we'll have a private 'quaint' cabin, complete with modern conveniences and an intensely productive three days of networking and motivational interaction while testing our mental and physical limits. Also, all meals, snacks and beverages are included. It goes on to say that once we enroll –and we must hurry because space is limited—the secluded and secret location will be revealed. I'm sure it's somewhere lovely and far away from the cold and snow. Maybe a remote tropical island! Give me your charge card. Mine is still, er, a bit over the limit. You can get reimbursed from the reward money."

Evi sighed and handed over her charge card. It seemed that Tami's charge card was always "a bit over the limit." The likelihood of getting "reward" money was a bit sketchy. The Wickiup Wine and Fudge Shoppe had apparently been the hiding place for an ill-gotten cash stash, which Evi had inadvertently freed from its hiding place in the Wickiup attic when she accidentally discharged a shotgun. In that the money was from a bank robbery of yesteryear, the confirmation of a reward was yet to be forthcoming. Especially when the feds were the ones who needed to fork it over.

However, a place without snow and cold and the prospect of a fancy drink with a little umbrella in and maybe some hunky guy in a grass loincloth giving massages was appealing. Plus, meals, snacks and beverages were included.

***

"This is your captain speaking," squawked over the intercom. "We welcome you aboard Appalachian Airlines and expect to arrive in Knoxville on time."

High On The Vine

While Knoxville, Tennessee was not the same as a tropical getaway, it would have been okay, what with the shopping and country music guys wearing cowboy hats and tight blue jeans. Trouble was, that was just the first leg of the Maki cousins' journey.

"Soooo," Evi said as she inspected the small cellophane-wrapped packet of peanuts that was to sustain her during the flight. "Once we get to Lexington, how far to Swampy Hollow?

"Well," Tami said, looking at the E-I-E-I-O website. We can rent a car at the airport, and I guess drive to Swampy Hollow in about four hours, depending on whether or not there is any snow in the mountain passes."

Snow. In the mountain passes.

"It says on the website that it is a good idea to rent a car with chains on the wheels and to pack emergency supplies," Tami said. "However, I do believe that Swampy Hollow is down in a, um, hollow so should be warmer and probably even majestic, what with the Smoky Mountains and all."

Evi's packet of peanuts burst open and scattered across her snack tray. She managed to recover most of them. Stale.

"And we will be staying in an authentic place called "Moonshine Lodge. My, I wonder if that is racist."

"What?" Evi said, as she struggled with the pull tab on her $7 beer.

"Moonshine," Tami said.

"How so?"

"I mean, isn't it marginalizing the community—identifying with moonshine, like they're all a bunch of hillbillies on a bender or something?"

"Dunno," Evi said as her beer fizzed onto her snack tray. She wondered if the moonshine came in a quart Mason jar. So much for exotic drinks with little umbrellas.

***

Women of the World Warriors (or not)

It was an arduous journey, to say the least. While the chains helped with traction of the Toyota Corolla rental, nothing could be done for the lack of visibility as they wound their way precariously down a narrow mountain switchback during a whiteout. Tami insisted Evi drive while she, Tami, attempted to engage the GPS on her phone.

RECALCULATING intoned the calm, yet annoying robotic voice of "Natasha" who proved to be as unsure as the Maki women.

TURN LEFT IN TWO BLOCKS

"Two blocks? This isn't a freakin' neighborhood!" said Evi. "And we're only going—" she glanced at the speedometer—"it isn't even measuring our speed 'cause we're going so slow."

TURN NOW! Commanded Natasha.

Evi jerked the wheel left, hit something, then jerked it right and hit the rocky wall of the mountain.

"Did we buy the extra insurance?" Evi asked, as she tried to control the fishtailing.

"Um, sure, I think so," Tami said.

RECALCULATING, Natasha said calmly. GO STRAIGHT FOR ONE HALF MILE.

"Straight! It's a hairpin turn. I saw the yellow sign barely through the whiteout..."

CONTINUE FOR...

"Shut that thing up!" Evi said.

"Wait! I think I see something!" Tami said pointing to a shadowy outline in the distant gloom.

TURN AROUND AND GO BACK! Said Natasha. DANGER AH, ACK!"

Then Natasha went strangely silent.

"I think that's it—the lodge—there in the, um, pretty snow," Tami said.

***

High On The Vine

"Welcome to Moonshine Inn, y'all!" bleated a very tall, very blond woman as the Makis emerged from their somewhat worse-for-wear rental. "My name's Atilla. Y'all come from a ways?"

Tami and Evi wrestled their bags out of the rental and dragged them through several inches of snow toward a long wooden porch that served as entrance to the "lodge," which more resembled a derelict homestead from "Deliverance."

"Er, yes, we've had quite a trip," Tami said, scrunching down into her parka in an attempt to discourage any more snow from going down her neck.

"Does it snow here often?" Evi asked.

"Why sakes no! Ain't it bah-you-tee-ful? We're so excited to have our first big snow in ten years! Why, it'll make our outdoor obstacle course a real hoot 'n a holler!"

"Obstacle course?" Evi said.

"Darn tootin'," said Atilla. "Now I'll get you ladies your key to your cabin and then once you settle in, y'all can come on into the gathering room for a meet up and greet and hep yersef to some good ol' down home cookin'. We lost 'lectricity with this storm, but no worries, we got a generator in the lodge and they's matches on the table in your cabin to light the kerosine heater and lamps."

With some difficulty, Tami & Evi hauled their suitcases into their cabin, which appeared to be lacking the promised modern conveniences.

"Do you think we could make it back to Knoxville, or even Pigeon Forge before dark?" Evi asked Tami as she stomped the snow off her boots.

"No. Too dangerous," Evi said while she fumbled to light a kerosene lamp, which flickered like a strobe light at a disco dance. "Besides, we Makis can handle a little snow. Plus, there are no refunds."

Women of the World Warriors (or not)

"It's freezing in here," Evi said as she squatted down and inspected the ancient-looking kerosene heater. "I thought the cabins were supposed to be modern."

"Well, Atilla did say they lost power because of the storm. Now buck up and let's go mingle at the meet and greet. I'm sure we'll find some others with start-ups like the Wickiup. Time to network!"

Evi did recall that there would be down home cookin'. The airline packet of stale peanuts was just a distant memory.

***

"What do you suppose that is?" asked Evi of a fellow WOWW participant. All attendees were given "Hello! My Name is___" badges. The badge of the woman Evi spoke to proclaimed her name to be Taralin, with a little heart drawn in for the dot over the "i." Evi was bending over the refreshment table, looking at some squiggly offering with funny little slug-like objects floating around.

"Whahl, I do believe it's blackeye peas and hog jowls," said Taralin. "They call it Southern caviar. Can you just imagine? Name's Taralin Milkford Wesson, by the way."

"Evi Maki."

"Pleasure," said Taralin. She eyed Evi. "Maybe you've heard of mah business: Taralin's Rejuvenation Sensation?" She paused. "They're beauty prahducts."

"No, can't say that I have," Evi said, eyeing another mystery food on the buffet table. "What's this?" she said, pointing to what looked like cooked seaweed.

"Whah collard greens, silly," Taralin said shaking her head. Now, if y'all will excuse me. But do considah tryin' mah products. They can work miracles!"

The only miracle that Evi was hoping for was to get the hell out of this place. Furthermore, there was no moonshine as far as Tami could see. How could a place be called

High On The Vine

Moonshine Lodge and not have moonshine liquor for its guests? Wasn't there a law about truth in advertising?

After the seven or so WOWW attendees had picked through the hog jowls, slugs and slimy greens, Atilla clapped her hands authoritatively. "May ah have your attention pahleez!" she bleated. "I hope y'all are enjoying our yummy buffet and meetin' greetin' tahnight. Now, tahmara we'll all meet here-ah at 5:00 a.m. before breakfast for our calisthenics and obstacle course run. Then a quick invigorahtin' group showah and hearty breakfust of grits and gizzards. Cookin' to die for, I declare! Now we're gonna take a vow of silence durin' the first 24 hours of this convention, startin' now, so y'all will jist need to keep yer questions and comments to yerselves for a spell.

"Five a.m.!" shouted Evi.

"Now, shush!" said Atilla.

"But how..." Tami said.

"I said shush. Understand?" snarled Atilla, causing the group of attendees to recoil.

"But..."

"Now, I have no tolerance fuh people who break the rules!" Atilla said, reverting back to her syrupy voice. "Understand, y'all?"

***

"Ladies and gentlemen, welcome to flight 2022, bound for Chicago," intoned the captain. "We have a little tail wind, so should be arriving at our destination ahead of schedule. Though we may have to circle around a bit before getting clearance to land. Anyway, please let us know if..."

"I have to say, Evi, you did a very nice job of driving last night through that snowstorm," Tami said.

Evi was gnawing on the wrapper of her complimentary granola bar trying to tear it open. She wondered if would be easier just to eat the wrapper along with the tasteless cardboard bar to ease the growling emptiness in her stomach.

"Of course, Natasha was a big help in navigating," Tami said. "But still, it took a lot of fortitude on your part to simply hug the granite cliff all the way up, then down that terrible road. My, but you did hug it!"

Evi nodded. It was true, she simply used the cliff wall as a guide while they climbed up then careened back down the mountain in the whiteout conditions. Of course, it may have put a scratch or two—okay, it kind of vaporized the driver's side of the Toyota. Fortunately, the rental desk was unoccupied when the gals returned the car, so they tossed the key on the desk and got in the line to board.

Evi was correct in her granola bar expectations. It reminded her of compressed sawdust. No beer was offered, perhaps because it was 5:00 a.m. Evi admitted to herself that she was actually looking forward to having a goblet of Monk Juice. After all, there's no place like home.

Full Circle

"Perhaps it's for the best," said Tami to her cousin, Evi. "I think the stuff had run its course."

Evi nodded. She was trying to suppress her elation as she pulled the little spigot on the fresh box of *real* wine, *not* the vile Monk Juice, which lacked palatability, but had proven to be quite flammable. The two Maki cousins were having a "reorganizational" BEEP (Business Enhancement Entrepreneurial Plan) meeting in the soon-to-be-renamed Wickiup Wine and Fudge Shoppe.

"Furthermore," Tami continued, "I have always felt a bit guilty snatching our husbands' hunting camp. After all, it had been owned by the Maki men for eons. I do feel the boys have served their penance for their horrendous transgressions."

While husbands Toivo and Eino had daily transgressions too numerous to name, the greatest calamity of all husbandly offenses was sending their wives on a vacation in the frozen tundra (something the Maki men won in a poker game) rather than a highly anticipated tropical getaway. While Toivo and Eino would carry the shame and blame of this for all eternity, Tami allowed that one must not be so blinded by rancor as to poison her own well.

Evi nodded again. It was best to nod agreeably when Cuz Tami spoke, though it often led to things like persnickety vacation renters, chickens, eggs, misogynistic monks peddling rot-gut wine and most recently the Women Warrior disaster. That little misfortune has set back Evi's credit card until Christmas in July.

"The monks say they'll rebuild, but I say not on our property. I mean they could have burned the entire forest down, along with the church camp across the lake if the wind had shifted."

"So, the Monk brothers are out of business?" Evi said as she popped a delicious piece of Tami's latest fudge, White Satin Cashew, into her mouth. It melted and blended perfectly with the slightly fruity hint of the box blush wine.

"I do believe the wine aspect of our store is more of a liability than an asset," Tami said, as she surveyed their shop. It contained everything touristy imaginable: local artisan crafts, coffee mugs and shot glasses, commemorative plates, books, tee shirts, goofy hats, supposed moose turds and bear scat encased in plastic, whimsical Northwoodsy doodads, wooden signs proclaiming a love of hunting, camping, cooking, grandchildren, saunas and all things Finnish. They had a sign on the front door that said Tervetuloa! which meant welcome in Finnish. And entire section of the store was dedicated to Tami's fudge (unquestionably way better than Island fudge) along with other treats and snacks including a much coveted (by Evi) chocolate/vanilla swirl soft-serve ice cream machine called The Confection-ate Cow.

Evi actually felt they did need wine in their shop and that *good* wine and fudge went together very well. Once customers had a complimentary swig of the alcohol, they tended to buy more souvenirs and such. However, the Monk Juice was God-awful and as far as Evi was concerned, good riddance. Had the Maki cousins been at all mindful, they would have sold the swill with a side of paregoric instead of fudge. The Wickiup Shoppe had some bad reviews on their website and at least one lawsuit pending because of alleged midnight gastro-intestinal issues caused by the Monk Juice.

"So, how do the Monk brothers think the fire started?" Evi said. She wondered how soft serve ice cream and wine would go together, if blended. Kind of like an adult milkshake. She imagined a sign in the front window: "Come have a Bo-Vine experience! Try our Wine-Cream shake!" (Must be 21 to purchase.) Of course there was the little matter of a liquor license.

"Well, according to Brother Barnabas, a very sinful now excommunicated monk whose name will remain unknown, was sneaking a smoke—and I don't mean tobacco—in the fermenting room. Who knew that wine fumes were flammable, just like gasoline vapor? Something about poor ventilation. Anyway, let's just say that the *joint* went up in smoke. If only he'd just settled for a gummy."

"So now the Bennie Violent Older of Silver Monks Winery is just a charred rubble," Evi said. Her brain seemed to be getting a little foggy and her speech somewhat muddled. In any event, she had to admit that it was very sad to see the pile of smoldering ash that had once housed the first (and hopefully last) Monk Juice faith-based winery. It had been a good building for livestock back in the chicken ranch days.

"I'm so grateful that we have good insurance," Tami said.

"We do?" Evi said.

"Well, the Monks owned the winery building," Tami said. "But we owned the cabin, which the Amish expanded considerably, and the other outbuildings—all piles of ash. Plus, do you believe it, they'll pay us for the trees that burned up!"

"No way!" Evi said.

"Way," Tami said.

"Hey," Evi said, "Time to open up the shhhhop." She went over to the front door and flipped the closed sign to open and pulled up the shade. When she looked outside an ominous dark vehicle pulled up to the curb. The last time such an ominous dark vehicle parked at the curb in front of the shop, a burly guy came in and demanded that the Maki gals turn over something left from the previous renter, Buck or Chuck or something like that. Turned out the burly guy was after a stash of cash from a bank robbery of yesteryear, which was inadvertently discovered after Evi blew a hole in the attic and freed the purloined bills. Without even consulting her cousin, Tami reluctantly turned the loot over to the authorities. There was some mention of a reward, in that banks were insured by the FDIC, but the cousins weren't holding their breath.

"Hey," Evi said, "ishant that fella that come lookin' for that stolen dough in jail now?" Evi had pulled the shade back down and was watching the car through a slit on the side. She could see it running but couldn't see in the tinted windows. Nobody was getting out.

"I believe he was, yes. However, they let them out now unless they have killed someone important."

"Wahl, I think itsh that car," Evi said.

"What car?"

"That burly guy's car."

Tami rushed over to the door and joined Evi peeking out the slit in the shade.

"Nooo," Tami said. "I believe that the bank robber's car was a black Beemer. That out there is a Chevy Impala and it's dark gray. Pretty dirty, too."

"Dang," Evi said. "If it isn't that burly guy, I hope it's not the tax guy." Evi suddenly felt very sober.

"You mean the IRS?" Tami said.

"Right, 'cause I'm not sure about some of our deductions," Evi said.

"Well," Tami said, "I thought the fellow who did our taxes was a CPA."

"Kind of," Evi said, " 'course Eino did win a free tax prep from him in a poker game, so, I'm not sure if he is one of them CPAs or just someone who does taxes out of the trunk of his car."

"Wonderful," Tami said. "That's all we need is an audit." She continued to peer out the slit of the shade. "Someone's getting out of the car. He looking at his phone and at our shop."

Evi peeked through the other side of the shade. "He's coming this way. He has a briefcase. I don't trust anyone with a briefcase. And he *looks* like a tax man. He has one of those thin little moustaches and a trench coat and he's tall and skinny and reminds me of a sharpened pencil."

The two cousins pulled away from the shade, flipped off the lights and scurried behind the counter just as pencil man tried the doorknob, which turned freely and the man stepped inside, blinking in the darkness.

"Why'd you unlock it?" hissed Tami.

"I didn't."

They both looked at pencil man as if he were supernatural.

"Hello?" he said.

"Er, you'll have to excuse us," Tami said. "We aren't open today."

"Excuse me?" said the man, squinting at Tami.

"Inventory," Evi said. "You'll have to come back some other day."

"I'm afraid that's not possible," said the man. "By the way, I'm Agent Snapps." The man limped across the room and offered an elbow bump.

"Tami Maki," Tami said as she engaged in the elbow bump. "And my partner's Evi Maki. Welcome to the Wickiup Wine and Fudge Shoppe.

"Excellent," Snapps said. "Just the two people I need to see."

"Er, we were going to file an amended thingy—you know ta ah ah... OW!" Evi blurted as Tami gave her discreet jab in the ribs.

"I beg your pardon?" Snapps said.

"How can we help you?" Tami said.

"Well, if I could just verify that you are who you say you are, we can conclude our business and…"

"Perhaps we need to VERIFY who YOU are," Tami said, stepping around the counter.

"Of course. My apologies," Snapps said, pulling a photo ID laminated card and badge of some sort out of his briefcase. He gimped a bit walking over to Tami as he presented her with the items.

"Horace Snapps. FBI."

"Wow!" Evi said, peering over Tami's shoulder. "I thought the IRS went after people for tax retur…OW!"

"I must apologize for the length of time this has taken," Snapps said. "You see, the case was so old and inactive, we weren't certain if the conditions had expired. You know, after all these years."

"Of course," Tami said.

"But we just filed OW!"

"Do you ladies mind if I sit down? I slipped on the ice coming out of my motel this morning and my ankle is killing me."

"Oh, well by all means," Tami said, directing Snapps to one of the bistro tables in the back of the shop. "May I get you a refreshment?"

Snapps looked around the shop and spotted the assortment of Monk Juice (there was some backstock). "Well, I'm not a coffee drinker…"

"We do have hot tea," Tami said.

"And wine!" Evi blurted out. "Monk Juice or boxed stuff."

"Monk Juice?" Snapps said.

"Yes, well, we will be fazing it out soon," Tami said. "An unfortunate accident."

"Well, I'm intrigued," Snapps said. "I wouldn't mind trying something called Monk Juice."

"Comin' up!" Evi said, ever eager to get rid of the stuff once and for all.

Snapps began spreading papers across the table. Evi set a large goblet full of Cross to Berry Monk Juice in front of the agent. Tami added a plate of fudge. Snapps absently took a swallow of the wine, jerked violently and nearly fell off his bistro stool.

"Holy cow!" he said. "What is this stuff? His gaze shifted to the plate of fudge. He took a square and popped it in his mouth. "My, a very odd combination."

Tami had put her cheater glasses on and was peering at the papers spread out on the table. Evi sloshed a bit more wine into the agent's goblet.

"So, anyway ladies," Snapps said. "Whoooweee, that stuff's strong!"

Tami felt her stomach lurch when the word REWARD jumped out at her from the legal mumbo jumbo.

Agent Snapps popped another piece of fudge into his mouth. "I shouldn't be eating this—or drinking for that matter. I have blood sugar issues."

"Me too!" Evi said.

"Eat your fruits and vegies," Agent Snapps intoned.

"Restrict your carbs. Blah, blah, blah!" Evi said as she refilled her glass from the boxed wine.

"Hell, I only got 22 months until retirement," Agent Snapps said, taking another hit of Monk Juice. "I'll be lucky to live that long, if I was to listen to the doctor, which I don't."

"I hear ya," Evi said, clicking her goblet against his goblet.

"Eh um," Tami said.

"Oh, wow, right," Agent Snapps said. "Back to business." He took another gulp and then ate a square of fudge. "What this is all about is that money you turned in a while back."

"Yessss?" the cousins said.

"The reward is still valid, but we of course have to cross all our I's and dot all of our T's." Snapps giggled and shook his head. "I mean dot all the T's and cross all of the I's."

The Maki cousins sat quietly, hearts racing. Reward! Tami envisioned enlarging the shop and hiring some help. Evi envisioned enlarging her house and adding an attached garage. Both women envisioned a luxury tropical vacation.

"So, um, how much?" Tami said.

"Well," Agent Snapps said. "Standard is ten percent of the recovery. I recommend that you spread out the payments over five years for tax purposes."

"How much," Tami repeated.

Agent Snapps removed some glasses from his shirt pocket and slipped them on his face. "Well, the recovery was two-hundred-fifty-three thousand, six hundred twenty-seven dollars. So, ten percent is..."

"Twenty-five thousand, three hundred sixty-two dollars and seventy cents," Tami said.

"Divided by two," Evi said.

"Less taxes," Snapps said. "Now if you took five thousand a year..."

"Forget it!" Tami said. "We want a lump sum."

"Very well. I recommend you consult your accountant immediately on this," Snapps said, as he polished off his goblet of wine.

"Let us give you a nice selection of wine for the road," Tami said. "That is, once you cut us the check."

"Oh, the sheck will be mailed," Snapps said. "First, I must have you sign a few thangs."

Full Circle

The Maki women huddled around Snapps and signed three times each, then initialed each page. Tami went into the tiny office in the back and made copies. She also pulled three bottles of Monk Juice off the storage shelf, along with a pre-packaged assortment of fudge and slipped the products into a "I (heart) The U.P." bag. She hoped this would expedite the check processing. When she returned to the shop, Agent Snapps was standing, but weaving precariously back and forth.

"I think my ankleshh better," he said. "I can't feel a thang."

Tami handed the agent back the original paperwork, which he tucked into his briefcase. She also handed him the swag bag.

"Thish has been a real pleasure, ladies," Snapps said taking the bag and peering inside. "This schtuff growshh on you."

The agent staggered toward the door, turned and gave a salute. "Feelin' fine!" he chirped.

The women waved amicably. "Wait until tonight," Evi said.

Epilogue
Turks & Caicos

"This is more like it," Evi said as she sipped a Piña Colada from a plastic coconut cocktail vessel. It came with two straws and a tiny umbrella with a chunk of pineapple skewed on its handle.

"Ahh, love that tropical breeze!" Tami said, also taking a sip from her faux coconut shell, which contained something called a pineapple Margarita, also replete with tiny umbrella and fresh pineapple.

Both of the Maki cousins were sprawled out on chaise lounges positioned in an open cabana thatched with palm fronds. A brilliant white sand beach stretched before them and merged with the crystal-clear turquoise waters of the Atlantic Ocean. While Tami wore a demure swim outfit that covered every square inch of her body, Evi had daringly stuffed herself into a low/high cut florescent floral number that could be seen from outer space.

Even though her eyes were closed, Tami sensed a presence hovering over her. She opened one eye and saw a person—a man, a young man who was wearing very little— smiling down on her.

"Hello ladies," said the scantily-clad man. "My name is Raul. I am your cabana assistant and am here to serve you."

High On The Vine

Evi's eyes had opened. She slurped the final vestiges of her drink and held out the empty coconut. "Nice to meet you, Raul. I'm Evi Maki and this is my cousin Tami Maki. This Piña Colada was very tasty, but this time please ask the bartender to put more rum in it." She slipped Raul a $50 bill. "You can keep the change if you keep them coming."

Raul nodded, a large grin spreading across his face. "And how about you Miss Tami, can I freshen you?"

Tami let the inuendo slide. She had no intention of giving some cabana boy a $50 tip—well minus the cost of the drink, which was astronomical. Plus, one of the cousins needed to stay sober so they could find their way back to their luxury suite, which boasted 1400 square feet of opulence and included two bedrooms, a Jacuzzi in the bathroom, a mini bar in the kitchenette and an ocean-view balcony. The Maki cousins had spared no expense in treating themselves to a very overdue and coveted luxury tropical vacation. They even flew first class to this glorious Caicos Island, which was about as far away as one could be from the snow and ice they left behind in Upper Michigan.

Raul departed to fetch Evi her drink. Evi enjoyed watching him from the rear. While she had no desire to let herself "wander" it didn't mean she couldn't look. She was darn certain that Eino did his share of looking at the cocktail waitresses at the casino. And likely he over tipped them, too.

Tami on the other hand failed to see anything of much interest in the departing cabana assistant, and more focused on what was on the agenda for the evening. It would begin with a colossal fish fry on the beach, followed by indigenous dancing and lively music. Tami did not intend on being hungover or drunk for this, as it was included in the resort stay and she liked to get her money's worth.

"So, what do you think the fellas are up to right now?" Evi said. Raul had returned with her drink. He did a curt bow, then sauntered off, sashaying as he went, giving Evi another good look.

The fellas in question were the gals' hubbies, Toivo and Eino.

"Well, I expect they are either using the $5,000 we gave them to rebuild their camp or, more likely, blowing it at the casino," Tami said.

"I certainly hope that if they are at the casino that they don't win any livestock or other crappy things," Evi said.

"Hey, how about we go snorkeling?" Tami said. "There's a class with an instructor starting in a half hour. I think the meeting place is around the boat house."

"I was thinking of a spa treatment," Evi said. "You know, with the oils and massage and a hottie guy."

Tami propped herself up on an elbow and studied her cousin. There was no denying that Cousin Evi was a bit of a tart. But she supposed it was harmless.

"Well, I guess we could go our separate ways. I'll snorkel and you get a rubdown."

"Massage," Evi corrected.

"Eventually," Tami said.

"Right, no rush. We have six days to do it all—and most is included!" Evi said.

"I wonder how the boys are doing," Tami said.

"Well, I left Eino a few things in the freezer," Evi said. "I expect they'll go the Legion a couple of nights anyway."

"I had to buy Toivo two extra packs of underwear. He seems to be unable to work the washing machine."

"Do you think they'll get cousin Heinkki to build them a cabin?" Evi said.

"Maybe," Tami said. "I think Toivo said they were going to buy a pre-fab garage and put it on a concrete slab."

"Garage?" Evi said.

"Yes. They are much cheaper than a pre-fab cabin. Of

course they could go in the woods, cut their own trees, strip them, notch them, build, chink and so on."

The two cousins looked at each other and burst out laughing."

"Riiiiight," Evi said. "Saw down trees—like with a chainsaw. I don't think Eino has started his in about ten years."

"Toivo lost his in a poker game," Tami said.

They both laughed again and said "pre-fab garage!" simultaneously.

"So, I wonder if Eino remembered that garbage goes out on Tuesdays," Evi said. "He always forgets."

"And to check the oil in Big Buck before he heads out fishing or hunting," Tami said. "It's been burning oil like crazy."

"Wait," Evi said. "Do you think we miss the guys?"

Again, the cousins looked at each other and burst out laughing.

"Yeah, Evi said, "Like a toothache. Ha ha!"

"Well, I'm sure they miss us—or at least nice meals and clean clothes," Tami said.

"Right, for sure. Hey here comes Raul," Evi said. I think I'll switch to wine. I wonder if we can just get a box of wine."

Fortified with another generous tip, Raul produced a nice box of wine, along with a cooler of ice to keep it chilled. He also provided the ladies with a tasty plate of snacks.

"Ah," Evi said. "No Monk Juice! I'd like to say that I miss it. NOT!"

"Well, Atilla said that she unloaded most of the backstock at the Wickiup, so I believe that we can put Monk Juice in the rearview mirror," Tami said.

"I was really surprised that Atilla was willing to give up her position at the Moonshine Lodge and come work for us," Evi said.

"Indeed. She is really quite the salesperson," Tami said. "Very persuasive. I believe we left things in good hands."

"Yup," Evi said. "Eino said he'd look in from time to time. Hey, what time is it at home?"

"Well, I don't have my watch, but I'd say around mid-afternoon there," Tami said.

"I supposed we could call—you know, just to make sure everything is okay. I do worry about the garbage sitting around too long."

"I guess it would be good to check in with them. Maybe at least send a text or a picture or something," Tami said.

"Or maybe talk to the lout," Evi said. "I mean, you know, see if the pre-fab garage thing is a go."

"Sure," Tami said.

"I'll get my phone," Evi said.

Tami's Peanut Butter Pinot Creamy Delight Fudge

Ingredients:

1 stick margarine
4 cups sugar
Can (12 oz) evaporated milk
1 & ½ bags (15 oz total) peanut butter chips
½ cup peanut butter
7 oz jar marshmallow fluff
1 t vanilla
6-9 ounces Pinot Noir wine
You will need 3 or 5 quart saucepan, 9 x 13 cake pan—greased with butter or margarine, candy thermometer, wooden spoon, rubber spatula, and large wine goblet.

To make:
Combine first three ingredients in saucepan. Cook over med/high heat until comes to boil. Stir frequently. Drink 2-3 ounces of wine
Cook at gentle boil (med heat) until reaches soft-ball stage, stirring frequently. Drink 2-3 ounces of wine.
Remove from heat and add peanut butter chips, marshmallow fluff, peanut butter, and vanilla, stirring vigorously. Once all ingredients are combined, immediately pour into prepared pan.
Drink 2-3 ounces of wine.
Cool and let set 6-8 hours or overnight.
Cut into 1" squares. Tip: Cut set fudge into four sections while in pan. Remove each ¼ section, one at a time, and place on waxed paper. Cut into 1" squares with pizza cutter or large knife. This is easier than digging each piece out of pan. Be sure to sober up before handling sharp objects!

About the Author

High on the Vine is one of three anthologies of humorous short stories written by Terri Martin. She also has two middle grade children's books and a full-length Upper Michigan mystery. Her stories often reflect the culture and characters she has encountered during her many years of living in the "Yoop" (U.P.). Terri and her husband enjoy watching the menagerie of freeloading wildlife from their home on the Silver River. While the winters are harsh, the soul never tires of the beauty of the Northwoods.

Martin has a master's degree in English and has taught college success courses, tutored English at the college level, and served as an aide for college composition classes. Her middle-grade children's book *The Home Wind* was a 2022 U.P. Notable Book recipient.

Visit Terri's website at www.terrilynnmartin.com or e-mail her at gnarlywoodspub@gmail.com

Tami and Evi Maki make a Special Guest appearance in Roadkill Justice!

Nettie Bramble lives with her ma in Upper Michigan in a cabin that's slightly off the grid. She claims to "subsist" off the land and prefers to do so without the benefit of hunting or fishing licenses. Nettie is bound to have a clash or two with the local woods cop, CO Will Ketchum, and the chronically cranky Judge Nightshade. Most places that Nettie goes, her "citified" nephews, Wanton and Wiley, tag along to muddle up her plans. Nettie will meet up with Church Lady Bea Righteous, as well as Tami and Evi Maki (thrice-removed cousins) in an erratic road rally with a cash prize that brings out the worst in everyone. No spoiler alert for the surprise ending in this collection of short stories featuring a strong dose of the Yooper way.

"Terri Martin writes fast-paced little tales peppered with humorous disasters following one after another... If you live in the U.P., you'll have heard plenty of fish tales and hunting sagas from your outdoor friends. Some of them may be whoppers, but none as big as the ones Nettie Bramble tells."

-- Jon C. Stott, author of *Yooper Ale Trails*

"Roadkill Justice's" unlikely heroine, Nettie Bramble, is rough-edged but 'big-hearted, with 'sisu' to spare. Author Terri Martin does a fantastic job of capturing the spirit and the spunk of the Northwoods character in a plot that sweeps her reader along, like a fast-running trout stream, on a delightful ride filled with twists, turns, laughter and the occasional explosion."

-- Nancy Besonen, author of *Off the Hook*

ISBN 978-1-61599-774-9

Modern History Press

A Disclaimer by Miss Bea Righteous

Well, my heavens! Where do I begin? First and foremost, while calamity may seem the result of my well-intentioned actions at the Gnarly Woods Senior Complex, I would like to make it clear that it is my mandate from above to protect the vulnerable, young and old, from taking that slippery slope into the devil's lair.

Perhaps inadvertent collateral damage has occurred but I must preface the recounting of my struggles with the devil and his minions by declaring that I am held harmless from any and all such incidental damage or harm.

Upon your wise purchase of this book (transformative!) and upon reading the chronicles within, I am fully confident that you will fully exonerate me from any wrongdoing and agree that I am on the path of righteousness. Though, of course, I do not expect any fanfare or meritorious recognition for my service

~ ~ ~

"Bea Righteous sees Satan just about anywhere and especially on those smartphones. There is no limit to how much damage Bea Righteous can invoke by way of her misguided do-gooder activities... a whirlwind of chaos surrounds our heroine... If this raises a chuckle, you are a definite candidate for the *Church Lady Chronicles*."

--Victor R. Volkman, *U.P. Book Review*

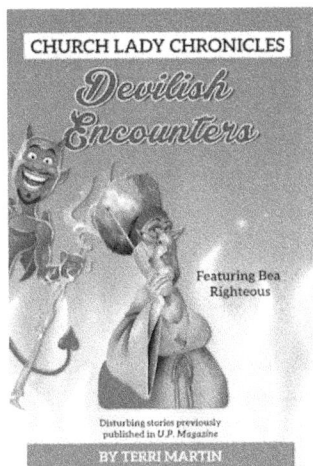

ISBN 978-1735-2043-0-7

Gnarly Woods Publications

A suspicious death in a game processing meat locker is just the beginning of bizarre events happening in the Upper Michigan village of Moose Willow. It all starts when a mysterious woman appears at the Methodist church during choir practice. Janese Trout and her best friend, State Trooper Bertie Vaara, team up to connect the woman to a growing number of disturbing occurrences around town including the disappearance of Janese's eccentric lover, George LeFleur, and an undeniable increase in Bigfoot sightings. Meanwhile, Janese faces a multitude of personal challenges as she grapples with a sagging career at the Copper County Community College, an elusive pregnancy test, and a controlling mother who inserts herself into every hiding place of Janese's life.

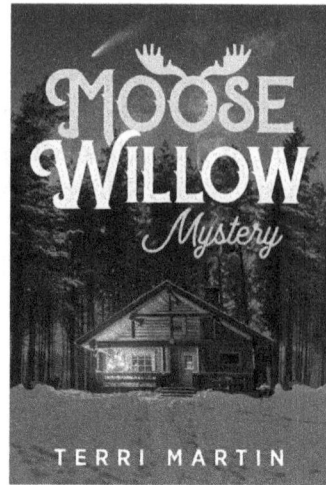

"*Moose Willow Mystery*, by Terri Martin, lets cozy mystery fans know they are about to experience something wildly different with edgy characters, a big dose of humor, and an insider's look at America's best-kept secret the mysterious Upper Peninsula of Michigan."

—Carolyn Howard-Johnson, award-winning writer of fiction, poetry, and the HowToDoItFrugally Series of books for writers

"Terri Martin manages to present the ordinary, the bizarre (of which there is a steady stream), and even the violent in a way that will open a hilarious glimpse into the world of a small town. With brilliant characterization, she takes the reader on a wild ride of murder and mayhem, so let me warn you. Don't start reading until you have the time to keep going."

—Bob Rich, PhD, author of *Sleeper, Awake!*

ISBN 978-1-61599-689-6

Modern History Press

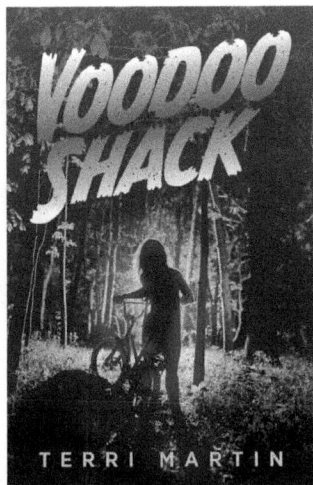

Join Iris and the Voodoo Shack gang as they investigate a mysterious death and an unsolved crime!

When 11-year-old Iris Weston discovers a ramshackle hunting cabin deep in Hazard Swamp, she and her friends decide it's perfect for a secret clubhouse. The gang dubs it the Voodoo Shack and meets there to swap stories and play card games. Ol' Man Hazard, the former owner, died under mysterious circumstances, and the kids speculate whether it was an accident, suicide or maybe even murder! The gang believes that cash from an unsolved crime may have been stashed within feet of the cabin. Even as things go badly awry, feisty Iris learns how to use her wit and independence to put things right, discovering what family really means in this adventurous and often humorous coming-of-age story set in rural Michigan in 1962.

"Set in the early 1960s, Martin's novel traces a girl's journey toward understanding the true meaning of love, family and friendship. Iris is an appealing character whose relationships with friends and family are realistically portrayed as she struggles to find her place."
--School Library Journal

"Martin has drawn on her childhood memories to create an engaging, feisty heroine, lively supporting characters and an easy-to-visualize early 1960s rural Michigan setting. And, although Iris doesn't solve all her mysteries, she finds the answers to the most important ones in this fast-paced story." *--ALA Booklist*

"Readers fond of lightweight mysteries solved by spunky heroines will take to this fiction debut, though a heavy ballast of tragedy and near-tragedy keeps it low to the ground. Some of the dialogue and set pieces show a promising authorial gift for comedy.
--Kirkus Reviews

ISBN 978-1-61599-720-6

Modern History Press

Jamie Kangas struggles with turbulent emotions caused by the death of his father, who perished in a logging accident--an accident for which Jamie blames himself. While his mother works as cook in a logging camp, Jamie is run ragged as chore boy. The grinding dreariness fades when Jamie meets a Native American boy, Gray Feather, who carries a burden of his own. The two boys become close friends as they face the challenges of a harsh environment and prejudiced world. And as trees fall to the lumberjack's blade, Jamie hears the ghostly words of his father, warning of future catastrophe.

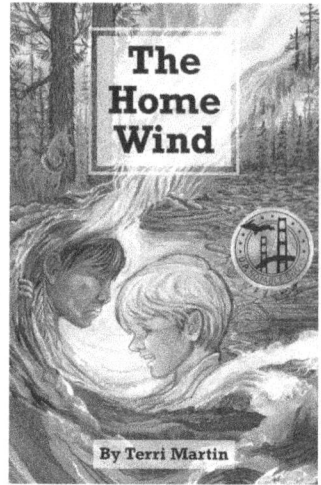

The
Home
Wind

By Terri Martin

The Home Wind is a middle-grade children's novel (ages 9 and up), which takes place during the 1870s in a Michigan logging camp. Quality paperback, 198 pages plus discussion guide.

"*The Home Wind* is a beautiful novel for both middle grade readers and a wonderful a read for adults, too. Steeped in carefully researched historical events in Michigan's Upper Peninsula, *The Home Wind* is a delight. Martin's characters captured my heart and made the story come alive--two boys struggling to understand the world around them. This is also an important book for anyone interested in the history of Michigan's logging industry and in the Native peoples of Michigan. I highly recommend *The Home Wind*, and if you are looking for a gift for your middle reader, it's perfect!"

-- Sue Harrison, author of *The Midwife's Touch*

"Martin's descriptions of the scenes and action make a reader feel as if they are right there in the middle of it all. Readers can't miss the symbolism found throughout the book and a wonderful way to learn about the past at the same time. This book should go far, and not just with young audiences." -- Deborah K. Frontiera, *U.P. Book Review*

ISBN 978-1-735-2043-1-4